THEY ARE MY SISTERS

They Are My Sisters

A memoir

by

SAMMY DYER

with Deb Dyer, Linda Hansell and
Mary Dyer Wilkinson

Adelaide Books
New York / Lisbon
2020

THEY ARE MY SISTERS
A memoir
By Sammy Dyer

Published by Adelaide Books, New York / Lisbon
adelaidebooks.org

Editor-in-Chief
Stevan V. Nikolic

For any information, please address Adelaide Books
at info@adelaidebooks.org

or write to:

Adelaide Books
244 Fifth Ave. Suite D27
New York, NY, 10001

ISBN: 978-1-951896-04-1

Printed in the United States of America

To the members of the L.I.F.E. Group, past, present and future:

your contribution to MY life is immeasurable.

Contents

Chapter One   *A Life-Changing Meeting* **9**

Chapter Two   *Early Influences* **16**

Chapter Three   *Life at the Shelter* **22**

Chapter Four   *Lives Intertwine* **26**

Chapter Five   *How Else to Save My Son?* **33**

Chapter Six   *A Life Sentence* **44**

Chapter Seven   *The L.I.F.E. Group* **53**

Chapter Eight   *Treasured Letters* **70**

Chapter Nine   *Lives Redeemed* **84**

Chapter Ten   *Josephine* **88**

Chapter Eleven   *Resilience and Strength* **110**

Appendix **117**

Appendix Endnotes **127**

Acknowledgments **133**

About the Authors **135**

Chapter One

A Life-Changing Meeting

It was the pink and white napkins that did it.

I was at a PTA meeting at Boulevard Elementary School in Shaker Heights, Ohio, the elementary school that all five of my children attended. I had been active in the PTA at Boulevard for many years. My youngest was now in sixth grade, and would be moving on to the junior high school the following year. At this particular meeting, we spent forty minutes debating whether to use pink or white napkins for the annual Teachers Appreciation Luncheon. Forty minutes! I thought, *you've got to be kidding me.*

I don't want to be critical of the PTA, but spending so much time on such a trivial detail got to me. I remember walking home from that meeting down Southington Road—we lived just a block from the school—thinking *there has to be something more meaningful I can do with my time. There just HAS to be.* I didn't know what that something more might be, but I knew I wanted to find it.

Later that day, these thoughts were still rattling around in my head while I was cleaning the house. My oldest daughter

Margaret was a student at Smith College in Northampton, Massachusetts at the time. She had recently told me I could throw out anything she had stored in her room at home. As I pulled things out from under her bed, I came across a poster for a "Runathon" Margaret and some of her friends had organized to raise funds for the battered women's shelter in Northampton. I remembered the event, and being surprised that there was a shelter in such a small and quaint college town. Something made me pause and I wondered if there was a similar shelter in Cleveland. Almost without thinking I found myself looking in the phone book, and I found the listing for Women Together, an emergency shelter for battered women.

I picked up the phone, dialed the number and asked if they had any volunteer positions available. I was pleased to hear they did and I was able to register on the phone that day for the next training session.

It was 1978. My five children ranged in age from 12 to 21. My husband worked in commercial real estate in Cleveland. As a housewife, I had always volunteered, usually in the PTA or at Metropolitan General Hospital. But now that my older children were in high school and college and my youngest was about to start junior high, I had more time on my hands and I was ready for a deeper commitment. I hoped the battered women's shelter would be the something more I was looking for.

Soon after my phone call, I started the two-week volunteer training workshop for Women Together. The training was held in downtown Cleveland at the YWCA. During the training, Jane—one of the staff members—told the assembled four or five volunteers, "We have our own guidelines for handling calls on the hotline and for our work in the shelter. The most important thing to remember is that this is totally anonymous. Never give anyone the address of the shelter, never give anyone your last name. And no sharing about anything that goes on here with your friends, your family, or the bridge club. We keep everything confidential, so batterers can't find their victims."

She continued, "Use this script to get through your first calls. If you take a call from a woman that wants to come in, you turn it over to me or Nancy and we'll set up a pick up. We have a few meeting spots around the city, public places like Burger King or a gas station that are easy for quick pick-ups in case the women coming to the shelter are being followed.

"Keep in mind," Jane continued, "this work gets pretty intense: you can't get emotionally invested. You need to protect yourself."

At the end of the session I approached Jane and privately said "I'm not sure how you can do this without some emotional investment – some kind of connection to put yourself in their shoes?"

"Trust me, I've been there, done that, and it doesn't work," Jane said. "It's much too exhausting, and it's not sustainable."

"You mentioned picking up the women who want to come in. Do volunteers do the pick-ups?" I asked.

"Generally not." Jane replied. "It can be dangerous if the batterer has followed the woman."

As I absorbed Jane's words, I felt that this was the type of challenging opportunity I had been seeking as I left the PTA meeting a few weeks earlier. And that was the beginning of what has now been my 41 years of volunteering with battered women in shelters and in prisons. Eventually I did do pick-ups for the shelter, and I became emotionally invested from the start. I understood Jane's wise advice, but there just wasn't any other way for me.

When I went to the shelter the following week for my first day, I was a nervous wreck. In spite of the training I wasn't sure what to expect, but I was willing to do whatever was needed. When the staff asked, "Would you mind cleaning the kitchen?" I replied, "Of course I don't mind. I'll do anything you need me to do." I wanted to help with something, even if it was doing the breakfast dishes or scrubbing the bathroom. I didn't care what I did. I just wanted to be of help in some way.

I knew I would have to answer the hotline at some point, and I was anxious about it. Luckily, I didn't have to do it on my first day. But a few days later, I was sitting in the office with one of the advocates—I think it was Jane—when the hotline rang. They all knew that I was pretty nervous about answering the hotline. Jane got up and said, "Oh Sammy, grab the phone, would you? I've gotta run to the kitchen" and I said, "Oh, uh, um, okay."

I answered the phone and on the other end of the line was a woman from an East Side Cleveland suburb who was very well off. She began telling me about her abusive husband. We talked and I told her about the shelter. She wanted to know where it was, whether it was downtown or some other location. I couldn't tell her the exact location, but gave her an indication of what part of the city it was in. She said she'd think about coming to the shelter, and I said, "Do think about it. I'm here on Tuesdays and Fridays, so you can always call. My name is Sammy. You can ask for me and we can talk again. You don't have to give me your address or name. This is all confidential. It does not go beyond this phone call." She called every week for a few months, and we would talk. But she never did come to the shelter.

My interest in volunteering grew, in large part, due to the young staff advocates working at the Women Together shelter—Jane Donnell, Mistinguette Smith, Nancy Olin, and others. I was in awe of their dedication to helping women, and inspired to be working with these young women who were the ages of my daughters. I tried very hard to suppress my urge to say, "Oh, Jane, honey," like I might say to one of my daughters. I was grateful that they didn't treat me like their mother or grandmother. I was accepted as a peer, and that was wonderful for me. I learned a great deal from these advocates about deep listening, the needs and challenges of battered women, and the methods that have proved successful in helping them. It was like getting another college education.

The shelter had a step-by-step-by-step process of helping the clients. I marveled at the staff's skill in handling some truly horrific situations that the women would reveal. I would be clenching my toes together to keep from crying. I'd say to myself, *Oh Sammy, don't cry, don't cry, do what the advocates are doing, listen, just listen.* The advocates did that beautifully, and I tried to emulate them. But I cried on my way home, or when I was walking my dogs. Hearing some of their stories, I began to be amazed by the courage the women had summoned to leave their abuser, often with small children, no money, no place to live, and no friends or family to help. Leaving was every bit as frightening as staying.

Domestic violence doesn't always come as a push, a shove or a beating. The abuse can be psychological as well. Many women told of their abusers saying things such as "You stupid, worthless, fat, ugly bitch. I'll kill you first, then the kids." The stories of verbal abuse were every bit as horrifying as the stories of physical abuse. Frequently there is both. I had a woman tell me that she thought that the psychological and verbal abuse were worse than having a broken arm, because the mental abuse stayed with her, stayed inside of her, and it made her question everything she did. *If I do this, what will he think? Will this make him mad? Is this the right thing to do? Am I smart enough to do that?* She said, "You start doubting yourself and your own abilities because your abuser has verbally told you that you are a dumb, stupid woman. A broken bone heals, but a broken spirit doesn't."

The psychological and emotional tolls of both physical and verbal abuse are extremely damaging. Good psychological counseling is needed to help people heal. It takes a lot of courage to seek out that help, and often women don't know where to turn.

When I started volunteering in 1978, domestic violence was not something people talked about much. There was a lot of excusing of behaviors. You'd hear people say things such as *Oh, he didn't really mean to push her down the stairs, she stumbled.* For many people, especially in my generation, women were used to having the man be the "top dog," the person that explains everything and is in charge. Many women did not feel they could challenge this, or that they had any options. This was true across racial, ethnic, and socio-economic lines. When I was a young woman it was not possible to pick up the phone and call and get help. I am encouraged to think that today women are more aware that there are places they can get help with issues of domestic violence.

At the shelter I learned that a battered woman trying to break free from abuse needs substantial support to find her way through the intimidating world outside the shelter or her abusive home. The staff at the shelter is constantly faced with figuring out what services each woman needs, and how to provide those services. The women need legal services, coping skills counseling, help with finding housing after leaving shelter, financial support, job search assistance, medical assistance, and child care. The list is almost endless. Sadly, most need support programs and counseling for their children, many of whom also suffered abuse. The staff advocates worked hard to customize support programs for each woman in order to help them succeed.

One of the women who ran the volunteer training, Nancy Olin—who would become a close colleague of mine over the years—told me many years later that when I showed up for that initial training session, all she and Jane could think was, *Oh boy, another one of those do-gooders from Shaker Heights.* Maybe it was my outfit—just what I usually wore—a long black skirt, white turtleneck sweater, bright red lipstick. I don't know if that's what prompted Jane's comment about the bridge club (I don't play bridge,) but I'm glad I succeeded in gaining their respect and proving their initial impression of me wrong.

Chapter Two

Early Influences

The early part of my childhood was carefree, growing up in the Detroit suburb of Ferndale, Michigan with my parents, Walter and Margaret Morris, and my older brother Donald. My brother Donald was six years older and I adored him. My full name was Sylvia Ann Morris, and with those initials I very quickly got the nickname Sam, and then Sammy.

My mother was a fulltime homemaker and my father was an executive for General Motors Corporation, the Assistant Director of Research and Development. Once, he was offered a promotion that included a free membership to the local country club. The discriminatory rules of the country club meant that his two closest friends—one Jewish, the other Russian—wouldn't be allowed in with him, so he turned it down. His boss was surprised, but my family wasn't. My father was a man of principle, and his friendships meant more than a promotion.

One of the things my dad told me many times as a kid was, "You are lucky to be who you are, and to be born into this family. It's not because you are funny, cute or smart. You are lucky." He also said, "You've only walked in your shoes, you've never walked in anybody else's shoes, so don't judge anyone for what they do, because you don't know what their life is like."

Another important lesson my dad taught me was that everybody has something special about them. Each person has some unique gift or talent, no matter who they are, where they live, or how much money they have or don't have.

I remember one day when I was about eight or nine I found my friend "Janie" crying in her back yard (our back yards were joined by a fence.)

"What's wrong?" I asked her through the fence.

She started crying even harder and said, "I just found out I'm adopted."

I had no idea what "adopted" meant but I didn't want her to cry, and as far as I could tell we were pretty much the same, so I said "Oh, that's okay, so am I!"

She stopped crying and that made me happy. She and I proudly told the other kids in the neighborhood we were both adopted. Eventually our parents heard about it and my parents sighed and said, "Oh Sylvia, you and Janie are very much alike. But you are not adopted." And they explained to me what adopted meant. It was then that I realized that my friend Janie's life had been harder than mine.

Not long after that it became even more clear to me that life was not as good for others as it was for me. The wife of the minister of our church organized a group of children to put on short plays. We were called the Drayton Avenue players as our church was on Drayton Avenue. We performed the plays at an orphanage not too far from our neighborhood. I had no idea what an orphanage was, and when we got there, my friends and I were in shock. The minister's wife explained that these children had no parents. I was upset to see that so many children didn't have a mom and a dad.

We brought homemade cookies and juice to share with the orphans after the plays. We loved that part, and had fun playing with them after the snacks. Afterwards we would go home to our families, and I always felt badly leaving them. I worried that when we went home it made them feel left out, different from us. I could see they were like me in so many ways; they just weren't lucky the way my friends and I were. I spent a lot of time thinking about this, and came up with a solution. I told my parents, "We need to adopt some of the orphans."

My parents said, "Oh, Sylvia, I don't think so."

"Well, why not? We have an extra bedroom, and I have another bed in my room. So, one can sleep in there and one can sleep in my room." I had it all figured out. It seemed so unfair to me that these children didn't have a mom or dad. But we didn't adopt any of them. This was one time when I didn't understand my parents' decision. I suppose that was when I began to realize that not everything can be fixed.

As a child I loved to read and learn new things. I enjoyed school and was always excited for the new school year to start. I asked so many questions my mother sometimes became exasperated with me. At those times, she would say, "Sylvia, would you like to go to your room to read a book?" These were magic words to me.

In the evenings after dinner my father was willing to entertain many of my questions, and engage in any sort of conversation with me, seriously considering my questions and answers regardless of the subject. I remember one night sitting with him looking up at the moon. I asked him, "Do you think anyone will ever go to the moon?"

"What do you think?" he asked.

"Well, how would they get there?" I pondered. And we talked for quite a while about how a person might get to the moon.

As I grew older and the world around me became more serious, so did my questions. I had especially difficult questions during and after World War II. I was in my early teens, and so much of what was happening was hard to understand. My brother was in Europe in the Air Force, and I followed the news constantly. Both during and after the war I asked my parents many questions about war, about life and death— questions with answers that made me grow up fast.

When Donald came home he would cry out from nightmares in the middle of the night, scaring me terribly, but he never spoke of the war. After college Donald left a guaranteed job with General Motors, finding his passion in art and becoming a successful art dealer. To me he was the epitome of strength and courage. He carried on with his life in spite of the horrors he surely must have witnessed during the war. He became his own person, resisting the pressures to conform to societal expectations.

Around this time, when I was about fourteen, my Dad gave me a book called *Peace of Mind* by Joshua Loth Liebman. It's a book about trying to find answers to the basic problems of human nature, and I've kept it to this day. I have my Dad's favorite passage, which happens to be mine too, bookmarked. The passage has helped shape my life. The page is a little worn because I've read it so often:

"Man is not a single self. He carries within him many selves – a happy self, a frightened self, an angry self. Man is like an omnibus with many little egos jostling each other as the vehicle of life hurtles down the highway. The great Jewish philosopher Saadia a thousand years ago pointed out this truth about our inner pluralism.... If we wish to achieve the good life we shall have to arrange for a democracy among our desires and interests rather than a tyranny of one over the others. There is a place for love, for food, for material security, for the achievement of wisdom in the happy life.... He says that a single color like yellow or blue is hard on the eyes and monotonous on the soul. Only mixed colors, blended together, produce the beauty of a painting. A single tone has only one effect and becomes discord and shrillness in our ears. It is only the mingling of different musical notes that can produce harmony and melody. If in the world of sight and sound, diversity is necessary, how much more in the achievement of the good life must there be a co-operative democracy of our instincts and our desires."[1]

It was the kind of thing my dad would do: offer up some guidance or throw a new theory or lofty idea my way. I would sometimes lie awake at night, thinking through our conversations about these ideas, these gifts, reasoning out things that I didn't quite understand. That made me feel very grown up and I loved that feeling, and him, dearly.

I began high school thinking about how important it is to recognize and accept our differences, always keeping in mind that everyone has something special about them. My favorite

[1] Liebman, Joshua Loth, *Peace of Mind,* New York: Simon and Schuster, 1946, pp.185-186.

times in high school were the times Donald was around and included me with his friends. I felt very sophisticated as Donald always treated me as an equal, giving me aspirations that differed from most women at that time. However, I did follow the more ordinary path for women and went to Albion College in Albion, Michigan. Different from most of my friends, I studied liberal arts rather than home economics. I loved being on my own at Albion, absorbing all the knowledge I could. After college I taught Kindergarten for five years before marrying and moving to Ohio with my husband, John Dyer.

My father's principles of equality and acceptance and my brother's example of strength and courage have stayed with me to this day. When I began working at the shelter with women who had been abused, and later at the Ohio Reformatory for Women, it was another reminder for me of the lesson my father taught me: not everybody lives the way you do, and unless you have walked in their shoes, do not judge.

Chapter Three

Life at the Shelter

I volunteered at the shelter twice a week and worked wher-ever needed—answering the hot-line, cleaning, organizing, sorting donations, or spending time with women who needed someone to talk to. When I first started volunteering, I wanted to jump in with both feet. Jane cautioned me not to get deeply involved with the women too quickly. The work of helping battered women, she told me, is not just about getting them away from their abuser. There can be multiple layers of dys-function and unhealthy patterns to work through. "There can be a fine line between helping and enabling," she said, "and sometimes the best way to help is to step back."

I think she said this, in part, because very often women re-turn to their batterer, only to be beaten again. This was always difficult to accept. We worked hard to follow up with them by phone calls and letters, but so many women just disappeared, no matter how hard we tried to help them start over.

As I began to get more comfortable in my work at the shelter, I took on more roles. I was asked to sit in on the meetings the staff advocates held with the women who had come to the shelter to get away from their abusers. I was impressed with the way they talked with the women and helped them get past denial without being confrontational or overly blunt. It was not uncommon for clients to deny the reality that their partner was a serial abuser. Many of them had grown up with abuse in their household, so they thought, *that's the way men are, aren't they?* A woman might say, "You know, he's really a good guy most of the time." And Nancy would reply, "Good guys don't punch their wives, right?"

The staff helped the women understand that what was happening to them was not their fault, and it was not something they had to continue to live with. The staff handled the conversations in a way that encouraged the women to take control of their lives. Many of them had never had any control. I admired the advocates' ability to help the women without any judgment, and without telling them "This is what you have to do," or "Don't do that." They cared for the clients' dignity.

Sometimes at these meetings a woman would break through and admit she had been denying that she was a victim of domestic violence. She began to realize that the problem wasn't that she didn't do the dishes properly, or cook the potatoes right, or some other thing her partner used as an excuse to beat her. Her abuser's behavior was all about control, and it constituted domestic violence.

Another way in which I was asked to expand my role was to go with women to different sorts of appointments outside the shelter such as doctor appointments, job interviews, or school meetings for their children.

I'll never forget the time I took "Susan" from the shelter to the hospital for a doctor's appointment. Her husband had been planning to take her, so he knew about the appointment and he was in the waiting room when we got there. He didn't say anything to her; he just sat there staring at us. Susan was shaken at the sight of him. She kept her composure but I could feel her trembling. I had her sit on one side of the room, as far away from him as possible and I went up to the nurse's station. I leaned across the counter and semi-whispered (maybe the drama queen in me came out just a bit), "I'm from the Domestic Violence Center with this woman on my left, and her husband is sitting over there in the blue shirt and the black pants. He wants to be part of this appointment. She's in shelter because of a domestic violence situation, and we do not want him to be in the Exam Room." I kept talking as if I were talking to a five-year-old because I wanted to be sure that she got the point. This was new territory for nurses and doctors at that time. The nurse was great. She said, "Yes, I understand."

As we walked toward the exam room he stood and started to follow us. The nurse turned to him, held up her hand and said, "We do not allow anyone in the Exam Room except the patient and their advocate" (pointing to me.) She was obviously making it up as she went along, and I thought, *Oh, thank God, she got it*. He glared at us but turned and sat back down.

When the appointment was over Susan was afraid to leave the exam room. I went out first to see if her husband was still there. Fortunately, he was gone. She was still shaken from seeing him and was afraid he was going to follow us. She waited by the receptionist desk while I looked outside to make sure he wasn't around. I had parked close to the entrance and we got to the car quickly. Susan locked her door and kept looking all around. She was worried he was still lurking around. I told her to duck her head down so he couldn't see her. I took a very circuitous route back to the shelter, making sure that he wasn't behind us. I doubled back and made all sorts of crazy turns to get her back there safely. She seemed to hold her breath all the way back to the shelter.

Today, when patients go to a doctor's appointment they are asked, "Do you feel safe at home?" as an initial screening question. In the early days of my work at the shelter this wasn't the case. Domestic violence advocates worked with hospitals and doctors' offices to get them to make that question part of their routine check-up.

Another memorable experience occurred when a policeman came to the shelter looking for his wife (who was there.) I answered the door and pretended to be a nun, telling him the building was a convent. He kept trying to look past me but I wouldn't open the door any further. He put his hand on the door a couple times - maybe he was thinking about pushing past me – and he was shifting his feet around, as if he couldn't stand still but was trying to hold himself back all at the same time. I kept thinking, *just don't move Sammy, just don't move one inch.* I'm not sure he believed my convent story but he did finally leave. Later we secretly got the woman out and over to Templum, the shelter on the West Side of Cleveland, so he couldn't find her. The staff at the shelter talked about that for a long time. I think they were more than a little surprised that this white-haired lady from Shaker Heights was able to fake out a city cop.

And then one day a woman came into the shelter whose impact on my life I could not have imagined.

Chapter Four

Lives Intertwine

I met Vanessa at the Women Together shelter in 1985. She was 19 years old and had come to the shelter with her 18-month old son. Vanessa was a pretty woman who clearly loved her little boy. I remember sitting on the steps in the hall of the shelter talking with her and holding her son on my lap. He was a little guy, so darling, and smart like his mom. I think I was one of the few people she let hold him or play with him. I didn't take that lightly, and I made sure I always asked her permission to play a game or read him a story. I think a lot of the women at the shelter felt they had failed as wives, mothers, even as women. I wanted her to know I respected her as a mother and as a woman. Mostly we talked about her son and her shelter stay, but we covered other topics, too, and I could tell she was bright.

Vanessa wasn't happy about some of the shelter rules, or the décor. Granted, the house and the furnishings were on the tired side, but everything was spotless and to my eyes it wasn't as drab or dreary as she seemed to find it. I loved the mostly-donated second hand furniture, throw rugs, mismatched plates, cups and silverware. To me it all had character and spoke of the many women and children who came and went there, making good use of it all.

As for the rules, it seemed that her main objections had to do with anyone telling her how to take care of her son. I hoped to help her understand that everything at the shelter was designed to take care of the children and make sure they were safe. I think she needed reassurance that he would be okay.

As I was talking with her, I kept thinking to myself, *she's 19. She has a child. She's in the shelter. My daughter Mary is 19 and she's in college. This woman is very bright, just like my daughter is very bright. What has made the difference?*

The difference was that Vanessa had been abused throughout her entire life, starting at age three. My daughter had led a life much like my own—stable, loving and not abusive. It was so striking to me that day to think of the differences between Vanessa and my daughter; once again driving home the lesson that so much of our early life, if not our entire life, depends on being born into one family rather than another. So much rests on whether or not you are born into a family of caring, loving people. Vanessa certainly had not had that luck.

When I went back the next week, Vanessa was gone. She had returned home to her abusive husband. I was sad that she left and I feared for her and her son's safety. In the short time I spent with her I had developed a genuine fondness for her.

As I mentioned, it was not uncommon for women to go back to their abusers. The shelter had a follow up program in which we called or wrote letters to women after they left. Sometimes we would hear from a former shelter client and she would be okay, sometimes not. I did a lot of this follow up work. Vanessa and I talked a few times on the phone, but a few months later, her phone was disconnected. This was not un-usual for our clients, some of whom moved frequently. Often our letters were returned to us as undeliverable. It was always heartbreaking when a woman just disappeared. We didn't hear from Vanessa for a long time, but I never forgot her.

In the fall of 1986 we received a letter addressed to Women Together with a return address from the Ohio Refor-matory for Women, the women's prison in Marysville, Ohio. It was from Vanessa, and that was how we learned that she was in prison for having shot and killed her husband. She wrote that her husband had been beating her toddler son with an iron chain and she couldn't get him to stop. She was sentenced to five to twenty-five years. She wrote to us at the shelter to thank us for all we had done for her. I was moved that despite all she had gone through before and after her time at the shelter, she wanted to thank us.

Around that time, several of the advocates at the shelter had been trying to get me involved in a volunteer program in the prison system called Man to Man, Woman to Woman. It matched volunteers with inmates and involved regular visits and communication, mostly through letters.

"Well, I don't know," I said. "I'm not sure that I would be any good at that."

"Are you kidding? You would be great, Sammy," they re-plied.

I hadn't considered it seriously before, but when I found out that Vanessa was in prison, it was a slam dunk for me. I wanted to see her. I contacted the people running the program to ask if they could guarantee I would be matched with Va-nessa. When they said yes, I signed up. I asked them not tell her she had been paired with me so that it would be a surprise when I visited her the first time.

For that first visit, the director of the Man to Man, Woman to Woman program took me to the Ohio Reformatory for Women (ORW). I wasn't nervous, but a few of my neighbors couldn't believe I wasn't scared to go there, or that my husband John would "let" me go. They felt the same way about my work at the shelter – they couldn't believe I would go "down there" to inner-city Cleveland for any reason. I thought that was kind of funny. It never bothered me, and John was always supportive of what I was doing. We never thought of it as unsafe.

On the drive to Marysville, the program director asked me if I had ever been inside a prison before. I told her I had not. She told me ORW was a lot like a college campus. I thought that was interesting and was eager to get there and see it.

The three-hour drive down to Marysville went quickly. We parked in the prison parking lot and started walking toward the main entrance. I looked around and thought, *well, you forgot to mention all the chain link fence with coils of barbed wire on the top surrounding the place.* It sure wasn't like any college campus I'd ever seen.

But it wasn't how I imagined it, either. I had pictured one huge building, but ORW was made up of several buildings, grouped to form a square around the grounds. The buildings were older, mostly brick and mortar. Each building had a purpose: classroom, meeting spaces, work-related functions, and some "cottages," where the women lived. I've never been inside a cottage, as visitors or volunteers are not allowed in.

A female Corrections Officer (CO) met us at the reception area. She explained that visitors have to hand over their IDs, have their coats, pockets and shoes searched and then go through a metal detector. No purses or bags of any kind were allowed in. After going through those security measures they stamped my hand and gave me a visitor badge. They told me I would get my ID back when I returned my visitor badge, and that they would check my hand stamp when I left.

We were buzzed through two sets of doors and met by another CO in the courtyard, who escorted me into the visiting hall. I followed the CO, eager to finally get in to see Vanessa. There were about five tables in the visitor's hall, each with four chairs. There was also an outdoor area with five picnic tables so people could visit outside in good weather. Visitors and inmates were allowed to hug and some held hands across the tables.

It was not an unpleasant room. Decorated with inmate's artwork, it was clear ORW had made an effort to make the room nice for visiting families and kids. There were vending machines that visitors could use to buy items for the inmates. Inmates entered from the opposite side of the hall and were searched before they entered, and again after they left, before going back into the "general population."

There were a few other visitors quietly talking to inmates in the hall when I took a seat at one of the empty tables. When Vanessa entered the room and saw me she cried out, "Sammy!!" We both started to cry as she ran toward me. We hugged, and she held on to me like she would never let go.

It was a wonderful reunion. Vanessa kept saying she couldn't believe anyone from the shelter had come see her. She was sure we were disappointed in her after she decided to leave the shelter. I told her we had been worried, but never disappointed in her for leaving. None of us judged her for anything that had happened. Vanessa started crying again, and I did too. We talked about how she was managing, and how thrilled she was to be paired with me in the Woman to Woman program. We also talked about her son; it was clearly painful for her to be separated from him.

We didn't talk about what had happened with her husband. Through my training at the shelter I knew not to ask, and she didn't bring it up. I didn't know if she would ever be ready to talk to me or anyone about it. No matter how much I wanted to help, I knew I would have to wait for her to be ready.

I started visiting Vanessa as often as I could. We wrote letters back and forth regularly. Her intelligence showed itself in her writing. One fascinating aspect of her writing was that she had two very different ways of expressing herself. Sometimes her writing was very articulate with an impressive vocabulary and command of grammar. Other times she would slip into what I thought of as her "tough girl talk," using a lot of slang, street talk, poor grammar, and profanity. She never spoke that way to me in person. I wondered if it were another version of herself; one she had created to help her feel strong enough to cope with the abuse she suffered. She seemed to go into her "tough girl talk" when she was describing situations where she was defending herself. Sometimes she used both styles in the same letter.

As we wrote to each other that first year, I couldn't stop worrying that she was holding on to a lot of trauma. We saw this often in the shelter, women who had not had the opportunity to process the trauma they had experienced. One of the tools we found that helped some women was to write down what they couldn't talk about. I thought this might be helpful for Vanessa as she seemed to really enjoy writing. I decided to ask her to write her life story in a series of letters to me. It took some time to convince her, but she finally agreed. I started by writing to her about when we first met at the shelter. I wrote a paragraph or two, sent it to her and then she was to write a bit about herself and send it back to me. We decided to keep writing back and forth like that to create her story. It became clear that she had a lot to say, writing pages and pages to me each time. From the beginning, she used up every piece of paper and envelope she was allowed to have, and was always asking if I could send her more paper.

Slowly, her story unfolded one letter at at a time. She has given me permission to share it here.

Chapter Five

How Else to Save My Son?

I was two months old when my mother disappeared. Since I have no memories of that time, I have to rely on, and believe, stories told to me by my father and others.

I was told that my biological mother was White and a prostitute, but she came from a good family. How she came to be a prostitute is a story no one knows. My father wanted to marry her but her family said no, most likely because he was Black. It wasn't money; in his day my father was a hard-workin' steel mill employee with no chemical addictions or interests. But he had his well-dressed, gangster-leanin', pimp, sugar- daddy side too. Maybe that's the side they didn't like.

He told me that in 1966 my mother left me in a sink in a vacant building after killin' someone, probably a "trick." My father said he found me with some of that intimidatin' gangsta shit of his.

When my mother disappeared on us, my father says he tried hard to change his ways, but the pressures of the world were too much for him to abandon his fucked up and unhealthy behaviors. People persecuted, ridiculed, accused and conspired against my father for having a blonde hair, blue-eyed "white" baby. In the mix of all that shit, my father found himself havin' to not only protect himself, but me as well. And believe me when I tell you that my father protected me at all cost…even the cost of others' lives.

For about two years my father's "women" took good care of me. When I was about two, he decided to move me in with relatives, either because his hoes was too tied down with me to make their quota, or just maybe my father wanted a better life for me. The move to the relatives' house was not a good one. My father figured that out pretty fast, but he couldn't move me right away. I stayed there for about a year. My father often found me wearin' nasty-ass clothes, shoes too fuckin' small for my feet; a Pamper filled with piss and shit…hangin' off my chafed ass, while playin' un-the-fuck-attended on the street curb.

I was locked in closets, the basement and the attic. My cousins' favorite game was to put me on the top bunk and make me jump or push me off, leavin' me covered in bruises.

There was a nice lady who lived across the street who gave me a pair of shoes that fit. I loved her for that. One day when I was maybe three years old, me and my father were sittin' in his car on the street and the lady came out and invited us into her home. She had two sons livin' with her, and two grandchildren. She and my father talked for a long time and the next thing I knew I was movin' in to her house.

I called the lady Granny, the same name the grandchildren livin' there used. Life was wonderful there and I was well loved by Granny, her husband, and her family. I felt like I was the same as them, part of a family for the first time in my life. My father visited often, spent extra time with me and brought lots of gifts.

Granny made sure us kids said our prayers every night before bed. I was made to sleep in the attic and say my prayers in the dark until I could say the prayer perfectly. I would cry for my father every night, but I never said anything to him about bein' put in the attic. Aside from a kinda mean nickname Granny gave me, things were pretty good there and I didn't want my father to take me away. I had decent clothes and shoes that fit, no more bruises from being thrown off the top bunk, and enough food to eat. I hated those attic stairs though. I'd sit there and cry myself to sleep while trying to concentrate and recite the perfect prayer. Granny just wanted us to be "good" girls. Once I got my prayers down pat, shit started lookin' bright again. No more attic!

From the start, one of Granny's boys took a "special" interest in me. He gave me a cute nickname and didn't use the mean one Granny gave me. He took me out for ice cream, candy and McDonalds, and let me get whatever I wanted. I loved it because I was not allowed sweets, and it made me feel special. When he started touchin' me in private places and doin' things to me, I didn't know it was wrong. No one had ever told me it was wrong for anyone to do those things. And I thought it was some kind of trade off for the sweets and the attention. We both got what we wanted. I'd have ice cream and he'd have me.

This went on for about two years, until I was about five years old. He did some things to me I cannot now or ever repeat. Things even in my young ignorance I knew were bad. I tried to avoid him as best I could. I think Granny knew somethin' was going on, but we never spoke of it. Maybe she stayed quiet to save her son. I stayed quiet so as not be labeled a "bad" girl, or be removed from the home.

I started kindergarten in the early 1970's when I was five. I went to the "Black" school. "Stuck-up," "trick-baby," "rich bitch," "yellow honky girl." These were the nicknames I was called by the dysfunctional-ass children who were my classmates because of my light skin and hair. I was badgered, talked about, and beat the fuck up.

Right around that time my father had become involved with a new woman. We moved into her house. It was her that decided I should be enrolled in a karate class to help me defend myself against the kids at school. I got kicked out of the class for kicking one of the kids from my school in the face. It was an accident, even though he deserved it. I didn't have the guts to do that to anyone, let alone a boy. After that, my father taught me the old school way to do things. He told me, "All you gotta do is pick up a brick and crack the biggest and baddest son of a bitch in the head and the rest will fall." I was about 6 years old at that time.

This new woman was in her late forties and was different from any of the other ladies my father had known. On one side she was plain yet sophisticated—petite and very lady-like. And on the other side she was a money-hungry, arrogant, spoiled and jealous-hearted slut. She owned her own home, worked in a beauty salon and had two sons. They were adults and lived elsewhere when we moved in. The story I heard was that she had known my father for years before they got together. Seems she was out to get him for a while; likin' his style and lovin' his money even more. I got along with her well enough, but she was really jealous of me. She was more interested in my father than the whole package. I called her mommy. I cannot tell you of the many tears I had cried wantin' a mommy.

I thought I had started to grow on her until we had our first "personal" conversation when I was about six years old. I asked the woman if she had any children. She said she had two and would have had three but one came out of her dead. I had no idea what this meant and it made me cry because it was scary. I asked her if it made her sad and she said no, because it had been a "nappy headed boy." She said she had really wanted a girl and that's why she was so happy she now had me. I was scared because I believed she killed her baby because it was a boy with nappy hair and I was the girl who took his place. After that I didn't interact with my new "mom" very much. I talked to her only when necessary; "yes ma'am, no ma'am."

The house we lived in wasn't very child friendly. Dark, drab and borin'. Her sons hung out there and smoked pot a lot so the carpet and furniture smelled bad all the time. My room had plain basic furniture, nothing frilly or fun for a little girl. When I complained to my father, he would buy me things, usually things beyond my years. Like a stereo system when I was seven. Nothin' fun to play with, but it did help me learn how to take care of my things at a young age.

I did my homework and played "single-mother house" with my dolls. I did really well in school even though I was bored, and was usually at least three chapters ahead of the class in every subject. I made merit and honor roll every quarter.

One of my new "mom's" adult sons, my sort-of step-brother, "James" and his friend "Marcus" hung around that house most of the time. They smoked pot all the time like I said, and made me smoke it sometimes. They did the same things to me Granny's boy did. By then I knew it was wrong but it was like I just didn't care I guess. It was just the way it was.

Marcus raped me a lot, but it was James who took my virginity. I was maybe twelve. My father would have literally killed him. I couldn't tell anyone…and it was an ongoin' thing. Until I left home. I set him up once, and told his mother to come upstairs in five minutes…she caught him. She didn't do anythin' about it. That's when I knew I had to get out of there. Nobody there was gonna take up for me, just like always. But she was the one time I got to call someone Mom.

I had just made the decision that I had to leave that house, but I wasn't sure how. I was walkin' down the street one day and a man I'd seen before was drivin' by real slow, watchin' me watchin' him. I'd seen him drivin' around—a well-dressed, handsome, and smooth Cadillac-drivin' man who carried himself with some respect. There I was, fourteen years old walkin' down the street, and there he was. We were like two magnets, I guess. He pulled over, got out, went around and opened the other door for me. "Hop in Princess." I knew I wasn't goin' back any time soon. The day I met him it felt like finally the rest of my life, the good part, was gonna get started.

I dropped out of school and for a time my life was the best ever. He had a temper, but nothin' too bad, just the usual couples-type fights I guess. By the time I was nineteen I had a two-month-old baby boy. We were still together. It was after the baby came that he became repeatedly abusive to me and my baby. I loved my baby so much and even though my life was far from perfect, I knew I would be the perfect mother. I would stop smokin' cigarettes and give up my occasional joint and breast feed him, because I knew that was the healthiest thing for my baby.

I don't know why, but my husband was strictly opposed to breast feeding. We fought about it all the time. I fought myself into more than one fat bloody lip over that subject. I think he was jealous of his own child.

After a few weeks of sneakin' around breast feeding, he caught me. It all happened so fast I barely had time to react. He slapped my baby out of my arms and by the grace of God he landed on the bed and not the floor. I was screamin' at him when I saw my baby's eyes rolled back in his head and blood comin' from his nose. He was turnin' a shade of grey I knew was bad. I panicked and grabbed him up and tried mouth to mouth even though I didn't really know how to do it. Nothin' happened so I called the paramedics but three minutes seemed too long so I screamed at my husband to get the car. We passed the paramedics on the way to the hospital and when we got there I was sure my baby was dead.

Then he made a little hiccup sound and his color started coming back. He was gonna to be okay.

The doctors had a lot of questions and I let my husband make up a story about what happened. They said it was SIDS, but I knew it was my husband.

My husband said he was sorry. Hell, I was "in love" and instantly forgave him by excusin' it all away in my mind as an "accident"…after all he was after my deceitful ass for breast feedin' behind his back, and not our precious, defenseless baby.

I wanted that closeness, that special bond between mother and baby that I had heard so much about, so I continued to sneak those breast feedin's until it became impossible. I knew I could survive the fights, the jealousy, the rage, blood, bruises and unwanted sex. I thought I was "in love." And anyway my parents had survived all that mess, so I could too.

Until he started to force me to ignore my babies cries and needs. I'd rather have my hands and feet amputated one by one than hear my baby cry and do nothin'. When my husband took my baby's face in his hand and shoved him back in his bassinet I knew I had to get away. I just didn't know how.

I didn't know about 911 back then, so I had to look up the number for the police department in the phone book. That's when I found the number for the battered women's hotline. At first I thought "Oh no, that's not me." And then I thought to myself "he fights you, beats you, curses you, cheats on you, and keeps you from your child – okay, maybe this place can help me." So I called the hotline, and damn, were they nosy. I just wanted someone to come get me while the gettin' was good. I ran out of safe time that first time I called, but the second time worked. I went with my son to meet someone at a McDonald's close enough that I could get to it with zero cash, and far enough away that he wouldn't see me there.

The people at the shelter were really nice, but I was so damn tired. I just wanted me and my baby to be left alone. I had to answer all the questions and fill out all the forms; all that procedure and formality shit.

There were a lot of women and children there. Some looked pretty rough with fresh bruises calling out "this is why I'm here." Some seemed well adjusted, maybe old bruises and hurts healed up. Me? I was scared... but I refused to let that show. Nobody was gonna know I had been beaten as senseless as some of these women looked. I thought that only happened to the weak, young and dumb. I learned later it could happen to anyone.

My room was okay, dark and gloomy but okay. It was on the third floor... I didn't like that. Reminded me of them attic stairs at Granny's. I was okay with the house rules and duties except for two. First off, residents were supposed to baby sit for each other if someone had to leave for work or appointments. No way was I leavin' my baby with a stranger, especially not a confused, mixed up, beat up and scared woman. Second, I was supposed to leave my baby in our room durin' meetings and classes – no way was I leavin' him unattended! Hell, if I had wanted to leave my baby like that I could've stayed home. But I couldn't go back to that mess.

I remember the day I met you at the shelter. We just sat there on the steps to the upstairs part of the house and talked while you played with my little baby, lettin' him crawl all over your lap. I remember we talked about nicknames because I had a silly one for my baby. And you said you had a silly one too, because your real name was Sylvia but everybody called you Sammy. We laughed about that. You were the one person in my life that gave me true comfort. You just let me feel like a regular person, not tellin' me what to do or what I did wrong.

After I was there about three days we had an educational meeting on the cycle of abuse. I followed the rule and left my baby in our room. I could hear him cryin' and it hurt me so bad I just couldn't stand it. I ran up and got him and brought him back down to the meeting. I didn't care about the rule, and that's what I told them. They kind of ignored it and went on with the lesson about the cycle of abuse. The verbal abuse, the physical abuse, and the honeymoon stage that follows it. I remembered how sometimes I would say or do somethin' to speed up the process to get to that honeymoon stage when I was the Princess.

Thinkin' about how much my man loved on me in the "honeymoon" times made me miss him so much. I had to talk to him. So I hung around after the meeting until I could make the call. Damn, he sounded good. He told me how much he loved me and missed me and our baby. He asked me what he had done wrong and begged me to come home. I got scared and hung up. But then I felt bad, and kind of wrong for hangin' up on him, so I called him back. He begged me not to hang up and that time he talked me into meetin' him the next day.

He looked better than ever. So sexy and dressed like a damn movie star. We just sat in his car and talked for a while. He kept askin' how the baby was. They really were happy to see each other. I told him the baby was good and had his routine check-up the next day. I started to get kind of nervous and decided I better walk back to the shelter. He didn't argue and I didn't give him any kisses or promises. But I sure did miss him.

The next day me and my baby caught the bus to the clinic for his check-up. When we got there I started to feel lost and afraid. I hadn't been anywhere besides that shelter without my husband since the day we met. I walked inside and damn, there he was. He found out the time for the appointment. I was relieved and a little nervous all at the same time. He called me Princess, carried the baby for me, openin' doors like he was trying to be a good daddy and a decent man. So we got all through the appointment and he was holdin' the baby the entire time, even when we walked outside. He offered me a ride and I said no thanks and reached for my baby. And then I knew what was gonna happen. He wouldn't give him back to me. Said he was takin' his son home and I could come with them or not, didn't matter to him either way. The way I saw it I had no choice. I followed my son...back home. There wasn't no honeymoon part this time.

Two years later, right before Christmas, was when everythin' changed for good, or for bad. I guess I'm still not sure. He came home one day drunk and ready to fight. He was furious because he had tried to call the house and the line was busy. I tried to explain I was just callin' the doctor for our son's next appointment like I had told him I was gonna do. He didn't believe me. The more I tried to explain the madder he got. He started throwin' things around the kitchen; picked up a knife and threw it at me, hittin' me in the leg. It wouldn't be the first scar he left on me. I was beggin' him to stop, if only for the safety of our son who was standin' so close. When he picked up his gun I started cryin' so hard I could barely see as I begged him to stop. Infuriated and crazed, he loaded a couple bullets into the gun, pointed it at me and pulled the trigger, burstin' into a crazy kind of laughter as I screamed and cringed.

My son was comin' closer to me and I was terrified for his safety. I thought if I could hide myself my husband would calm down. Sometimes it worked. If I, the object of his extreme anger, was out of sight he would forget to be angry. I managed to slide along the wall toward the bathroom until I was able to duck in and lock the door. It was quiet for a minute. Then I could hear him yellin' at my son. When I heard my son start to scream I knew my plan had failed and I ran out of the bathroom. Horrified, I saw him beating my son with a chain. My only thought was that

I had to stop him. I tried jumpin' on his back. Outraged, he tossed me off his back and shoved my son into the wall. As I ran to try to scoop him up he hit me across the side of my head. I fell to the floor. Lookin' up I saw him goin' back toward my son. Without thinkin' I got up, picked up his gun, aimed and fired. I didn't know how else to save my son.

Chapter Six

A Life Sentence

Vanessa's story, with its multiple layers of physical abuse, neglect, and sexual assault starting at age three, broke my heart. When I read in her letter that she thought the sexual abuse by Granny's son was some kind of trade off for the sweets and the attention he gave her, I shuddered. Many women at the shelter thought this way—that the abuse was okay because of the gifts or special treatment they usually got after an incident.

I was infuriated by the fact that Vanessa and many other victims of domestic violence had been abused and neglected as children by the people who were supposed to be protecting them. But more than anything I was struck by her strength and resilience in the face of the repeated abuse she had endured.

Vanessa was tried and convicted for killing her husband and sent to the Ohio Reformatory for Women, where we reconnected through the Woman to Woman Program. She had had a second child after she left the shelter, a baby girl, and both children were placed under the guardianship of the man who claimed to be Vanessa's father.

Vanessa had never had any structure or responsible adult authority figures in her life and early in her incarceration she complained about and challenged some of the rules and regulations at ORW. I think she would agree now, however, that the structure and rules helped her navigate through the prison system and create the best life for herself that she could within those walls. It was a more stable life than she had ever experienced on the outside. At least at ORW she knew she would have food, a bed to sleep on and clean clothes to wear. And the chances of being beaten were pretty small.

I began to understand why, although she learned to respect the rules and authority of the prison system, she was not likely to ever truly accept them. I think that would involve a degree of trust she could not allow herself. This helped me see why she always wanted to challenge things, and why she had been so protective of her son when they had been in the shelter.

In the beginning, Vanessa wrote a lot about her father. I think she created a version of him that helped her cope with everything that had happened to her. She wanted so badly to believe that he was the one adult in her life that had not abused and abandoned her. I suspect that was not the case. In 1989 she wrote to me that her step-mother called her and unceremoniously announced "your daddy is dead." Vanessa said she hung up on her. She never mentioned him again.

There was one other woman, who I'll call Joan, who visited Vanessa regularly at ORW. Joan had been married to Vanessa's abusive step-brother, "James." She divorced him because he was abusive to her as well. Joan visited Vanessa as often as she could from the start of her sentence, even before she divorced James. After being at ORW for a while, Vanessa wrote to Joan and told her what James had done to her when she was a child. Vanessa wrote to me:

I was so afraid to tell Joan, but I did. And she's written me back to tell me she doesn't hate me. I couldn't imagine life without her.

Vanessa gave me Joan's phone number, so I called her to arrange that we could go to the prison together. Joan couldn't afford a baby sitter so she brought her own kids and we would pick up Vanessa's son and daughter. Joan and I visited Vanessa with the kids many times. Vanessa loved seeing her kids, even though it made her very sad when it was time to leave.

Much later, Joan and I would spend a lot of time with Vanessa's children outside of those visits. There were many home care, school, and health issues, and they needed a lot of help. It was a lot to manage, so Joan and I worked on it together. Upon her sentencing, the children had been placed under the guardianship of Vanessa's father and step-mother. Joan and I checked on them at that home, and reported unsafe and unsanitary living conditions to the Child Services Board (CSB) many times. Her daughter had serious health issues, having been diagnosed with sickle cell anemia, and I frequently took her to doctor appointments.

Joan and I got to be very good friends, and stayed in touch over the years. I remember she told me she could never give up on Vanessa, or blame her for anything that had happened. Vanessa didn't have anybody else and had never been treated right by anyone. It was just that simple for Joan. Vanessa later told me that she would have been lost a long time ago if hadn't been for Joan and me, the only two constants in her life.

Vanessa seemed to thrive during her time at ORW. She received her GED, and then in 1989 she got her Associates degree from the University of Urbana through one of the educational programs at ORW. Her first parole hearing was in the fall of 1989, almost four years into her sentence. I had kept the staff at Women Together up to date on how she was managing in prison, and everyone was rooting for her. Two advocates and the executive director wrote letters to the parole board in support of her release. I think those letters, along with the documented facts of the abuse of her son at the time of the shooting, helped with her case. She had a pretty good record while in prison, having taken advantage of the educational opportunities available to her and trying her best to follow the rules.

She was granted parole in 1989 and transferred to the county facility. It was called "pre-release" and was supposed to help transition offenders out, but it was really just the county jail. I visited Vanessa as often as I could to help her with her plans once she got out of there.

Vanessa regained custody of her children not long after her release, and she and I were both overjoyed about their reunion. Vanessa's original plan was to move in with her step-mother. She changed her mind, however, as she became more and more nervous about running into any of her dead husband's family in Cleveland. I understood this, but I was very worried about her new plan to move to Akron where she would have to build a new support system. She said she had friends there who she could stay with until she found a job and a place to live. Joan and I didn't think that was a very good idea, but she had made up her mind and there was no stopping her. As long as she stayed in Ohio she was not in violation of her parole.

We stayed in touch for a while after she moved to Akron, and she seemed to be doing okay. After about a year, though, I lost track of Vanessa. She stopped answering the phone or responding to my letters. Joan didn't have any luck contacting her either.

Then, in 1995, Joan did get news of her, and it didn't sound good. Vanessa's step-mother had called Joan after Vanessa contacted her asking for money. Apparently, Vanessa had three more children now, two boys and a girl, and it wasn't clear who the father was, or if there was more than one father. Joan said Vanessa was either living with, married to, or just friends with a man more than twice her age who was living on disability. It was all very unclear. Other than that, Joan didn't know much, but she promised she would let me know if she heard from her again.

In the fall 1998 I heard from Joan again, and the news was bad. Vanessa had been arrested and charged with the murder of the older man that she had been involved with. Vanessa had become heavily involved in drugs and had gone to this man's house to borrow money. He refused, and as they argued she became afraid and grabbed a metal pot from the kitchen and hit him repeatedly in the head. I also learned she had been the subject of several other police reports alleging violent behavior on her part, but no charges had been filed. She was found guilty of killing this man and sentenced to fifteen years to life. She went back to ORW in Marysville, Ohio. Her three youngest children were placed under the guardianship of the man who claimed to be their father. He refused to accept responsibility for the older two and they were placed in group homes.

I was stunned and heartbroken. Vanessa was so darn bright, and had done so well during her time at ORW. I had hoped she would be able to create a new life for herself, one free from violence and drugs. But my work at the shelter had taught me how difficult it is for women to break the cycle of abuse and to overcome early trauma and neglect.

When Vanessa began her second term at ORW, I was volunteering with the L.I.F.E. Group there, a support group for women serving life sentences. I was not able to visit her, as volunteers are not allowed to visit offenders who are not part of their specific program. I could, however, write to her, and by early 1999 she started writing me back. I'll never forget one of her first letters from that time:

> *When I put you on my contact list it pained me so much to have to put "friend" when all I wanted to put down was "mom." I always think about what my life would have been like if you HAD been my mom. Maybe I would have had a sister, or at least a brother who didn't touch me. And a Dad. A real family. I could have gone to college, studied to be a doctor or teacher. I love you so much. I just hope I haven't pained you too much with my burden.*

She started to call me Mom or Mommy, addressing me in her letters this way. She also would sign her letters "Your daughter, Ann" giving herself a new name. I think she was trying to create an alternative reality in her head to help her cope with being back in prison, just as she had with the memory of her father.

Her words reminded me of what my father always told me: "You were lucky to be born into this family. The only thing that separates us from others who are less fortunate is luck. We aren't any better than anyone else."

She was deeply ashamed of what she had done. I think she felt that if she had been the "good girl" she was supposed to be these men would have treated her better and none of the violence would have occurred. Many battered women feel this way; if only they had tried harder, cooked better, cleaned better. Vanessa, and others, don't see that the deck was stacked against them from the start. It devastated her to lose her children. She had wanted so badly to be the perfect parent. She felt as if she failed miserably at the one thing she wanted to succeed at most.

I encouraged her to apply for membership in the L.I.F.E Group at ORW. They were a strong and caring group, and I thought the support would be helpful to her. And we would be able to see each other.

Her next letter was both hopeful and wistful:

They are helping me with my placement in the L.I.F.E. Group, and other groups and programs. How often do you come for the meetings? If I ever get in I will be starving for your attention!! This helps me now when it seems the darkest ever. This is worse than before, I guess because he was truly a good man who was maybe my only friend. I feel shame to have ever thought he would hurt me in any way.

No matter what I've ever done, you have never turned your back on me. I'm sorry to have ever disappointed you.

The only thing I could do was continue to write and reassure her that I was not disappointed and would always be there for her. We continued to write. In early 2001 she got into the L.I.F.E. Group. The group had very strict standards and codes of conduct and it wasn't unusual for admission to take time. When she finally got in, I was so excited to finally see her. She wrote to me after that first meeting:

Well, I've finally stopped crying long enough to be able to write. You looked so beautiful today and everyone in the Group loves you so much, including me. I wish we could have had more time, but I'm so very grateful to have seen you, even if it means sharing you with the Group. I've missed your great hugs so much, and didn't know how bad I needed one until I was in one.

We stayed in touch for the next sixteen years. As before, Vanessa seemed to do well in prison. She participated in many offender volunteer groups such as mentoring new offenders, decoration committees for special functions, dog training, and she maintained her status in the L.I.F.E Group.

After 2011 her letters dwindled, but we saw each other at L.I.F.E. Group meetings every month, and she always put me on her list for Family Friend Day, which was held twice a year. Around this time, she stopped calling me Mom, at least in her letters. She would still refer to me this way occasionally at meetings, I think as a way of trying to show other L.I.F.E Group members that she was closer to me than anyone else. She also stopped referring to herself as Ann. I like to think that she had come to terms with who and where she was and decided she was ready to get down to the business of creating a life for herself where she didn't need to pretend anymore.

In 2017, Vanessa applied for a transfer to a different county facility which was rumored to be less crowded and quieter. Her transfer was granted. I had known she was thinking about doing this, but she had not told me she had actually gone through with the process. Once she moved I couldn't contact her, due to the rules of the Ohio corrections system which don't allow a volunteer to contact any inmate outside of their volunteer program.

A year had passed without a call or letter from Vanessa, and I missed her. As I began working on this book, I reached out to her through the corrections system, and I was able to get permission to see her at her new facility. We had a tearful reunion, as we have been friends for over thirty years. I was grateful for the chance to see her again. I know she is still deeply wounded and troubled by her past, but I also sense that the inner strength and spark of resilience she has always had is still there. I am hopeful this will help carry her through. I hope that I can continue to visit her. I think of her often, usually when I wake up in the middle of the night. She wrote to me once that she thinks of me in "the wee hours." We used to laugh about that, how we felt like we were the only two people in the world awake in the middle of the night. I would like to laugh with her about that again.

Chapter Seven

The L.I.F.E. Group

After visiting Vanessa in prison at the Ohio Reformatory for Women (ORW) in Marysville a few times during her first incarceration, I received a phone call from a Marianist religious brother named Joe Clark. He had gotten my name from Diana Cyganovich. Diana had developed and was managing the first legal advocacy program at Templum House, the battered women's shelter on Cleveland's West Side. I had met Diana on several occasions at meetings and conferences.

When Brother Joe called me he said, "Diana Cyganovitch gave me your name as someone who is well versed in domestic violence issues. I've been meeting with a group of women at the Ohio Reformatory for Women (ORW) in Marysville, many of whom are victims of domestic violence and are serving life sentences. We're in the process of putting together some focus groups for these women centered around how to apply for clemency. Would you be willing to come and speak with them at one of the focus groups we are planning?"

"Actually, I already go to Marysville as part of the Woman to Woman Program," I told him.

We had a long conversation about the L.I.F.E. Group, the support group for women at ORW who were serving life sentences, in many cases for killing their batterer. Given my relationship with Vanessa, this idea really caught my attention. When Joe asked if I would be willing to speak with the group, I was a little intimidated, but I told him I was interested and would definitely like to know more.

Joe explained that the L.I.F.E. Group was started in 1987 by a case worker named Rebecca (Becky) Cardine who understood that being sentenced to prison for life is psychologically very different than being sentenced for a fixed amount of time. The fixed-timer, who has a sentence of say five or ten years, comes into the prison and begins counting the days until she will be released. But when a lifer starts serving her sentence, she can't count the days. She is confronted with the prospect of being there for the rest of her life. What does she have to look forward to? To hope for? Becky Cardine knew they needed something to keep hope alive.

Even though lifers had this additional set of needs, they didn't have the same access to rehabilitation and enrichment programs as the general prison population. To address this issue, Ms. Cardine started the L.I.F.E. Group. She wanted the lifers to be able to organize themselves into a group to support each other and to be productive. She wanted them to have projects and plans to look forward to. L.I.F.E. is an acronym for "Looking Inward for Excellence," a phrase created by one of the founding members of the group, a woman who is still incarcerated. Initially there were about 10 women in the group; at the time of this writing there are 100. The women are able to talk about their difficulties, share insights and strategies for how to "do time," and support each other.

Equally important, they are involved in numerous charitable and benevolent causes and plan positive social activities.

I agreed to go to a L.I.F.E. Group meeting with Joe. We were joined by Willa and Frances who were also volunteers. Frances, originally from Detroit, had been a battered spouse who had managed to escape in the middle of the night with her children. Willa was formerly an inmate at ORW who applied for and was granted a commutation of her life sentence. I soon learned that they had a close bond with the women at Marysville. And we would soon become very close ourselves. Our trips to Marysville would become some of my favorite memories.

There were only twelve women from the L.I.F.E. Group at the first meeting I attended. We sat in a circle, quietly talking—so different from meetings now! I felt an instant connection with the women in the group, a feeling of common humanity. I never had a feeling of being afraid of anyone or of the group. I thought to myself, *why are these women here? I could be here if I had walked in different shoes.* It was as if my father were there with me, reminding me how lucky I had been.

Joe lived in Dayton at that time and Frances and Willa lived in Cleveland, so it was easier for the three of us to drive down together and meet Joe there. The meetings were held in the evening, and the six-hour round trip drive gave the three of us the time to become very, very close friends. During those six hours we three would solve all the problems of the world! Willa worked full-time and had to get up at the crack of dawn to go to work, so often on the way home she would fall asleep.

There was one drive home I will never forget. Willa was in the back seat as usual so she could take her evening nap.

Frances and I were talking about, of all things, whether we would want to be cremated or buried when we died. Frances said she couldn't stand to be buried because she was claustrophobic and couldn't stand having anything covering her head and face. I said I couldn't stand to be cremated because of my work volunteering in the burn unit at Metro General Hospital. Just as we were starting to talk about what other options there might be, Willa piped up from the back seat, "You two are just crazy!" We all laughed so hard I almost had to pull over!

In 1993 our volunteer group expanded to include Mary Dwyer,[2] who Joe had met in 1988. As a young woman, Mary had joined a religious order—The Marist Missionary Sisters—and became a registered nurse. She served much of her young adulthood in South America, the West Indies and Jamaica. She and Joe became the closest of friends and ultimately both left their respective religious orders so they could marry. Mary's warm and compassionate nature made her a perfect fit with the L.I.F.E. Group volunteers. The women accepted her wholeheartedly from the start.

The L.I.F.E. Group is run by the women themselves, along with an ORW staff advisor. It has an Executive Board made up of a President, Vice President, Secretary, and Treasurer, as well as standing committees to manage administrative needs, advocacy, education, and programs. Each standing committee has a chairperson. Individuals are nominated, and the members of the group vote in elections every November. Not everyone with a life sentence can join the group. Members have to apply, and they have to have, and maintain, a clean record in prison. They have to respect confidentiality as well; if someone is a

---

[2] No relation to Mary Dyer Wilkinson

blabbermouth, they won't get in, or stay in, because what's said in the room has to stay in the room. Trust and respect are hard earned commodities in prison, and the women in the L.I.F.E. Group guard both carefully. If either is violated by a member within the group or outside of the group, they can be asked to leave.

In the early years, the group meetings consisted of having outside speakers, sometimes attorneys or advocates for battered women, but more often religious leaders, entertainers, or self-help experts. The goal was to find speakers that would represent a variety of issues and ideas. After several years, the activities of the L.I.F.E. Group expanded.

The women in the L.I.F.E. Group do an extraordinary amount of volunteer work, including a significant philanthropic component. They started out selling popcorn to raise money, and have expanded into selling submarine sandwiches and ice cream. They sell the food to the general prison population and ORW staff. With the money they earn, they support programs that assist people in prison as well as charitable organizations outside of the prison. Funds are also used to put on events such as Family Friend Day. Between 2002 and 2011, the L.I.F.E. group donated a total of $154,557 to charitable organizations. By the summer of 2017 the group had been in operation for 30 years and had donated just over $300,000.

Within the prison they have donated funds to help with recovery services, family services, education, graduations, inmate health programs, horticulture, juvenile incentive programs, and programs to assist incarcerated veterans. Organizations they have supported outside of the prison, either with financial contributions, hand-made items, or donated supplies, include:

ABC's Nursery at ORW (baby quilts, clothing)

AIDS Taskforce, Cleveland

American Cancer Society

American Red Cross

Appalachia Help

Baby Bundles for CAMO in Honduras

Bethlehem Store

Boy Scout Troop 873

Burial Gowns for NICU Unit, Metro Hospital, Cleveland

Central Ohio Hugs Program

"Change the Cycle" Walkathon

Children's Hospital (baby items)

Children's Services

Crayons to Computers (school supplies,
book bags, pencil pockets)

Crop Walk

Department of Veterans Affairs

Domestic Violence Shelter

Edgewood Elementary School (Book bags, pencil pockets,
puppets, flash cards)

Eugenia Theatre for Inner-City Youth

Faith Mission

Gables Nursing Home

Girl Scout Troop 4140

Katrina Relief

Literacy United

Make a Wish

March of Dimes

Marysville High School (banners, murals)

My Very Own Blanket (blankets and quilts for children in the Ohio foster care system)

Ohio Historical Society

Ohio Literacy Council (murals and banners)

Ohio Reads (murals, banners)

Ohio Wildlife (blankets, covers for cages)

Project Hope (Haiti Relief Fund)

Providence House, Cleveland

Relay for Life

Responsible Family Life (baby quilts, clothing)

Ronald McDonald House (baby items)

Salvation Army

Second Chance dog Program (dog kennel mats and coats)

Sew Much Comfort (For veterans at Walter Reed Hospital

Shriner's Hospital

Susan G. Komen Breast Cancer Fdn.

Take It To The Streets

Trinity United Methodist Church

Tsunami Relief Fund

United Negro College Fund

United Pentecostal Church

Veteran's Hospital, Chillicothe, Ohio

Vineyard Church

Volunteers of America

Warm Up America (quilts, blankets, winter wear)

Wings of Hope (quilts, blankets, winter wear)

Wings of Hope Foundation

Group members also participate in a project called Community Group Dues (C.G.D.) which involves community service hours. This is a way for members to pay dues in a non-monetary fashion that is beneficial to self, the group, and the entire ORW community. All L.I.F.E. Group members are expected to obtain at least 50 hours in a calendar year. These women truly understand the importance of working for the greater good. One of the most amazing experiences I've had at ORW was attending a gospel choir concert that was organized and directed by one of the women in the L.I.F.E. Group, and performed by other members of the group. The concert was incredibly beautiful. I asked her afterwards, "How did you learn to conduct a choir like that? It's amazing."

She said, "Well, my mother made me go to church with my grandmother every Sunday, and church lasted all day long. As a teenager I really didn't like that. But then I got here, and I started thinking maybe I could start a choir. And I started thinking about all the things you have to do to start a choir. You know, I listened to my grandmother's church choir all day, every Sunday for as long as I can remember until I got here. I just pulled on all that."

I was impressed, both with the concert and the kind of change that a person can make within themselves to adjust and adapt to life in prison. Many of them become productive, empathic women who develop skills and talents they never knew they had. I think it takes a long time to develop that level of grace in yourself.

I am also moved by the way the women in the group treat each other. It's not all roses-and-sunshine, but I have seen many instances where a woman has taken care of another woman who is upset, or who has lost a family member. When somebody new comes in with a life sentence – especially when it's a young woman—the women in the L.I.F.E. Group try to help her spiritually, help her feel that her life is worth something. The caring and compassion that they show to each other is a very important part of who they are. They are so much more than the crime they committed.

They're now in a situation where they can try to be the best person that they can be, the person underneath the horrendous things they have experienced all of their lives. They're finding out who they really are. They've told me what their childhoods (and part of their adulthoods) were like—brutal, traumatic, filled with abuse, violence, and drugs. Nobody should have a childhood like some of these women had.

My experiences with the L.I.F.E. Group have made me grateful for my life, and humbled. And always brought me back to what my Dad told me many times about not judging anyone unless I have walked in their shoes.

I've always felt that saying a simple "thank you," or giving someone a smile, or doing anything that could make somebody feel a little bit better, is like giving a gift to someone. And it requires so little effort. I remember when I volunteered in the burn unit at Metro General Hospital and the smallest kind gesture meant so much to the families and the burn victims. I've found this to be true at ORW, where each woman is so grateful for just a smile and a kind "hello."

In 2014 the group developed and started their bi-annual event they call "Family Friend Day." Each member of the group can invite four family members or friends for a full day visit. They organize outdoor games for the children such as kickball or basketball. If the weather doesn't cooperate they hold games and activities inside. Hula hoops and bean-bag toss are popular with the kids, and recently they set up a manicure station. They bring in food from an outside vendor for breakfast and lunch, and take pride in decorating the tables.

At the last event I attended they decided to try a cook-out style lunch which they cooked themselves, and it was terrific. I've been to Family Friend Day many times, and it's always wonderful to the see the women with their families, especially their children or grandchildren. They are always eager to introduce me to their family, but I don't want to take time away from their being with their loved ones. Sadly, some of the women don't have anyone to invite. The women look out for each other though, and usually those with no one visiting get invited to join another's group. So they become part of a family, at least for one day. Over the years this event has grown, and is now always at full capacity of 400 people.

In 2018 the group started having workshops on how to prepare for parole hearings, in which the women do mock interviews to prepare for meeting with the parole board. They also put together informational study packets covering what to expect and how to prepare for a hearing. This is another way in which they support one another and give each other hope for the future. Together they work hard to create a meaningful life on the inside, at the same time working together to keep hope alive for a life on the outside.

Once a year ORW holds a prison-wide volunteer appreciation dinner at which they give a Volunteer of the Year Award. ORW counts on the L.I.F.E Group to help coordinate setting up the room, decorating the tables and putting together the gift bags for the volunteers. In 2017 the L.I.F.E. Group began preparing the food as well, and their assortment of gourmet appetizers and desserts rivals that of any restaurant! I've enjoyed meeting other volunteers, and have been inspired by hearing about the work they do. Twice I was honored by the L.I.F.E. Group for my volunteer work, but I told them we should be honoring them for all the good work they do inside and outside the walls of ORW. These women have taught me so much about accepting life with grace and dignity. Any time I face what seems like an insurmountable obstacle or problem, I think of what these women have had to deal with, and how much they've accomplished in spite of the terrible hand they were dealt. They are my well of strength and inspiration.

For the lifers, figuring out how to manage a life sentence is a process that can take many years. As Joe wrote in a letter reflecting on his many years of attending L.I.F.E. Group meetings,

> "Most of the lifers enter the prison as angry young women. One can spend one's entire lifetime being angry: angry at family, angry at the judicial system, angry at themselves. But eventually some can realize that they are there, in prison, and not somewhere else. And the one asset they have is time. For these persons, slowly the anger subsides and courage emerges. Life becomes a search best characterized as a search for self. It can be spent looking inward for excellence and can release talents that have been there all along, but have been obscured by abandonment and a lack of love. Simply put, there is much time to figure out who one is, if one wants to use the time that way."

Over the years I've seen this process of transformation in many of the women in the L.I.F.E. Group. For some of them, the religious groups that come in and hold services are a life saver. For others, being involved in community service projects helps provide focus and breaks the routine of their everyday lives. And for many, it's the simple fact of being accepted into a community of caring people who, for the first time in their lives, don't judge them.

The women are immensely talented. Their achievements are impressive and wide-ranging: writing and directing plays, writing short stories, organizing a gospel choir, working for their parole, obtaining an engineering license, a GED, or an Associate's degree, learning Spanish, sewing, quilting, painting, cosmetology and organizing exercise classes. They have not lost hope. They will sometimes say, *When I get out, I want to be ready. I want to be the best person I can be.* They don't give up and they keep their hope alive.

Sometimes it takes a while for their talents to emerge, and for them to trust enough to share them publicly. I remember going to a L.I.F.E. Group meeting one day and talking with a group member who I'd known for seven years, and who had told me about her traumatic childhood. That particular day she told me she hadn't slept well the night before. When I asked her why not, she said, "I couldn't get the ending just right to the story I'm writing for my nieces."

"I didn't know you were a writer," I replied. "You never told me that before."

"Sammy," she said, "it's hard for me to learn to trust."

Her response could have been that of many of the women.

There are a lot of rules and regulations at ORW and that can be a big adjustment for the women. Many of them had no structure in their childhood, no family stability, and some of them learn to value having structure and rules. One woman told Joe that being in prison was the first time in many years she didn't have to figure out every morning how to avoid getting beat up. Knowing that there is a sameness to their routine they can count on is helpful, even if it's only the fact that once a month people like Willa, Frances, Mary, Joe and me walk through the door to see them.

The fact that these women are counting on us is motivation enough for us to always go to the monthly L.I.F.E. Group meetings, unless we're sick or there's a snowstorm or other terrible weather. At the end of one visit a group member told us, "You know, we're sitting there and, all of a sudden, the door opens and you came, you all walk in. And I just can't believe it and I'm thinking, oh look, they came back again. They really care. About us. They make us feel human."

Each of the five of us volunteers—Frances, Willa, Joe, Mary and me—brought something different to the group. Frances was a battered woman and so could relate well to the other women had been battered. Willa, of her own accord and through a lot of research into the laws, won her appeal for commutation of her life sentence. She served about ten years of her sentence, and upon her release knew she wanted to "give back to the sisterhood," as she put it. Among other things, Willa assisted women in writing up their cases for clemency applications. Mary was born with a depth of compassion that has no bottom, and the women instinctively know they can trust and rely on her.

Joe has a strong sense of right and wrong, fair and unjust. He lends a sense of quiet, firm support these women have never before experienced, especially from a man. He is very aware that many of the group members have had only very bad experiences with men, and therefore lets each woman determine how much, if any, interaction they will have with him.

As for me, well, I just try to listen carefully and be ready with a hug when needed. I enjoy talking with them. Some of the women would rather talk to one of us than to one another, and that is always fine. Both Frances and Willa are African American. Joe, Mary and I are white. The L.I.F.E. Group is racially mixed, and currently is comprised of sixty-nine percent white women, twenty-five percent African American women, and six percent who describe their race as "other."

Sadly, Willa and Frances haven't been able to visit for a number of years due to medical issues that prevent them from making the trip. Many in the L.I.F.E Group remember them fondly, and know that both are always with them in spirit. I myself missed a lot of meetings after I had a stroke in August of 2017, but I've started going again and it's so wonderful to see everyone. I missed them. Right after my stroke I couldn't speak, so my daughters gave me pen and paper so we could talk. I was worried because there was a L.I.F.E Group meeting the weekend after I had my stroke and it didn't look as though I would be able to go. One of the first things I asked my daughters to do was to call Clara Golding-Kent, the Warden's Administrative Assistant at ORW, to tell her I wouldn't be at the meeting and ask her to tell the women how sorry I was that I wouldn't be there. When they heard about my stroke, the group sent me the most beautiful card.

There are a lot of new faces in the group, and to be honest I have a little trouble remembering their names, but it doesn't seem to make a difference. They know me, and all that matters is that I come back.

It's always hard for me to say goodbye to the women at the end of a meeting, hoping they're going to be alright, hoping they can manage the day-to-day living for the next four weeks. I gradually got to know how hard it is for them. I've learned that there is a harsh reality to life inside any prison that most of us will never know. It's hardest at night when they're trying to fall asleep. The weight of feeling "I will be here the rest of my life" is pretty heavy, and that's one of the reasons the women get involved with the community service work that they do. It helps them to help other people.

The L.I.F.E. Group celebrated its 30th anniversary in 2017. I was thrilled to be at that meeting. The group has become everything Becky Cardine envisioned, due to the hard work and dedication of the members as well as continuing support and guidance from Clara Golding-Kent. She goes above and beyond the call of duty, and is highly respected for her level of commitment and her firm-yet-fair approach. She is, and has been for many years, the guiding force behind the L.I.F.E. Group.

The women in the L.I.F.E. Group at ORW in Marysville have taught me so much about grace, acceptance, and forgiveness. I have great respect for them and all that they do. As I've gotten to know them and they've gotten to know me, I have come to feel that they are my sisters.

I wrote this poem in their honor. I was very moved to learn that each member was given a copy after I had my stroke.

The Women of Marysville

They are women who have a number
but that is not who they are
They are women with deep wounds
inflicted when they were little girls
They are women struggling to deal with those
issues and the issues that brought them here
They are women with dignity
They are women with courage
They are compassionate women
They are women with feelings
They are women who love
They are women who are angry
They are women who are sad
They are women who cry
They are women who grieve
They are women who, although their days
are gray, can manage to laugh
They are mothers separated from their children
They are grandmothers separated from
their children and grandchildren

They are women imprisoned by darkness, yet
see light at the end of the tunnel

They are women who are teachers
They are women who knit, sew and crochet
They are women who sweep floors
They are women who cook and bake
They are women who study academics and computers
They are women who make flags and lenses
They are women who plant flowers and paint flowers
They are women who write poetry and music
They are women who sing and dance
They are women who train dogs
They are women who are beekeepers

They are women who are involved in
community service projects
They are women who organize events for charities
They are women who graciously welcome
you when you visit them
They are women who talk to God or a Higher Power
They are women who do not talk to God or a Higher Power

They are women who are Looking Inward for Excellence
They are women who look deep within
themselves and find their souls
They are women of color
They are white women
They are women
They are the women of Marysville
And they are my sisters

Chapter Eight

Treasured Letters

After I had attended the L.I.F.E. Group meetings for a while, it came to me that another way I could support the women would be to write to them individually, as I did with Vanessa. Gradually, as I got to know the women in the group I told them they could write to me anytime, if they wanted to. I was really pleased that so many did write, and I responded right away to each letter I received. This letter writing became one of my favorite things about my volunteer work with the L.I.F.E. Group.

I usually wrote in the evening when the house was still and quiet. It was a joy to write to them, even the hard letters, trying to encourage a woman who was struggling with something. I would mentally put myself in ORW, and envision I was at a L.I.F.E. Group meeting with the woman I was writing to. Perhaps it was wishful thinking, but I always hoped she could sense I was thinking of her at that exact moment, and that it would somehow help her.

Some women trusted me enough to share feelings of despair and the pain of being thought of as less than human by people on the outside.

"All too often we are made to feel like something one finds on the sole of their shoes."

~

"According to society anyone serving a life sentence is nothing but a drooling mad dog that should be shot. ... if only they could come to know the women as I have come to know them."

~

I hoped that my letters would give them a feeling of being seen, of being known, of being heard. To know that they are worthy of love and respect. Joe said this kind of written interaction gives the women a chance to feel ordinary rather than incarcerated, because we are peer to peer when writing letters to each other.

I was always touched when I would get a response. Even with everything they had to cope with, the women would always ask how I was doing. I've saved all of their letters, and I keep them in large plastic bins under my bed so I can feel closer to my friends.

Occasionally they shared feelings of missing their families, though not often. I suspect for many it may have simply been too painful to share.

> *"Thank you for calling my parents. My mom is so very ill, Sammy. I'm so frightened I will lose her before I do get home. It's important for me to share the love I have for her and to let her feel that, regardless of how she abused me growing up, I accept her and still love her today. I can't tell you how important it is to me to share that forgiveness with her. It's a healing we both need and I pray God gives that chance."*

> *"First let me say that not only do I trust you bring my mother down to see me, but it would be an honor to have you do so…any arrangement you and my mother make would be more than okay with me. I haven't seen her in so long, I would imagine I'd have trouble recognizing her. Though I know in my heart that if she were wrapped in gift paper sitting in a corner with her back to me, I would recognize my ma."*

> *"Thank you and everyone else for your Christmas card. It's a rough time for me to be away from my family. It's so painful there's days I wonder if I'm going to make it. How could I allow a man to do this to our lives? It's a question I don't think I'll ever hear an answer to."*

Sometimes their letters spoke of their efforts to adjust to prison life, or being unable to adjust.

"I am trying my best to wrap my mind around the fact that with the additional time and attitude I will never leave here as long as I am alive."

~

"I deeply appreciate your concern about my well-being and that of the others who have been here for lengthy periods and undergone so many negative changes. I am sort of like a willow tree in that I bend almost to the point of breaking but so far have been able to regain my strength and stand tall again."

~

"I feel so helpless just waiting. I need outside help in order for me to leave this place. It's not easy living from day to day without being able to help yourself. This is the first time in my adult life that I ever had to depend on others. Never put yourself in that position."

~

"I guess you heard by now that one of our sisters ended her life New Year's Eve. It is sadder to give up all hope of ever leaving here but sometimes our length of time is overwhelming. We've got to always look for that ray of light even if it's a faint flicker from time to time."

~

"My 31ˢᵗ birthday has come and gone. I would be lying if I said it hasn't affected me. I'm quite depressed. When you entered this place a child it's quite difficult to look at your face and not be sad. Older, and yet absent of all the experiences your constituents were afforded. Not that I really believe my life would have been better. I would

probably be dead if it weren't for coming here. That is just another sad reality of this."

Often the women wrote of lessons learned, regrets that they feel, and reflections on their lives.

> *"A day never goes by that I do not regret and feel deep sorrow for the poor choices I made in the past and the traumatic effect those choices had. I cannot change the past but please look at the person I am today and the potential for good I possess."*

> ~

> *"I need educated and professional people to fight for me to help the Parole Board understand how I could have killed him. Why I did what I did. They don't get it and I can't explain it. I did something totally out of character*

that even I don't understand fully. The best way I can is to say I know now how a cornered animal feel, and that the instinct to survive and protect your young exists in human beings as well. I've felt it and it's real and over powering of any good sense."

~

"I would like very much to talk face to face with you. There is a lot I can tell you, too much to put on paper. I was truly a mental, and physical(ly) abused woman for 25 years. My husband was a dog. He raped my sister, would hit or shoot at anyone. Threaten my life as well as my family's life. I was sexually abused, why did I stay with him, simple fear and love all at the same time. It is so hard to explain my feelings."

~

"'Why didn't you just leave?' Leave and go where? He was everywhere and he was invincible. I did leave and my (child) was kidnapped by him. I went back. I did leave; he stalked me at the grocery store. I did leave; he paged me constantly over and over day after day on my work pager. My customers heard him and his insane rantings. My boss threatened to fire me. I went back."

~

"I am serving a 23 years-to-Life sentence. I will have lived as many years here as I did before I came here before I even have my first parole board hearing. I have remained silent for nearly 12 years about my life, but now I am looking for a voice. I want to save my life, and hopefully make a change so that no other child EVER feels as desperate as I did all those years ago."

It breaks my heart that this next letter was written to me in 1999, and this woman is still incarcerated in 2018:

"I believe in my heart I have utilized the facilities offered within the system to the best of my ability to further my education, vocational skills, social skills, spirituality, and my awareness to give back to society. I am currently enrolled in the 8,000 Optician Apprenticeship program. I plan to parole to a halfway house given the long period of time I have been in prison so that my parole will be a positive number in the statistics. I know that the "nature of the crime" can never change, but the person convicted has, and in my case for the better. Would time change the past, then each minute I serve would be so worthwhile. I made poor choices and will carry this knowledge and deep remorse with me the remainder of my life. Women statistically convicted of a violent offense make the best prisoners as well as the best parolees. I know I am not a threat or danger to anyone, and have a great deal of positive attributes to offer society if I am afforded the privilege of parole."

~

Many women wrote about their desire to help other battered women:

"Sammy, I have such a burning desire to share my life's testimony with the women in shelters upon my release. I hope you will help me do that as soon as I get home. I can help so many women love themselves and at the same time save lives that don't have to be lost because of the insanity. My tragedy could be someone else's saving

grace. What a wonderful thought that is and I'm so excited and serious about making a difference out there Sammy. It could save an abuser's life, not only a battered woman's. My regular job will be my financial survival and my volunteer work with battered women will be my soul's revival."

"I would be happy to do an interview with _____ for her dissertation. Sammy, I don't care if it helps me with my board hearing or not. I stand on faith my path is freedom-bound. It may help a battered woman out there and that means more to me than freedom. Sparing another this insanity is my duty... As unjust or unfair as it may be that I'm here, it was designed for this very purpose. I am who I am today because of my time here. I prayed every day to die, instead God sent me here to live and save lives later."

"I am not ashamed to admit that I have...(an) ENORMOUS DREAM that I hope to realize. If I am blessed enough to achieve it, I plan to give back to young abused women by instilling in them an ability to see themselves for the powerful individuals they are."

Sometimes their letters were uplifting, full of positive growth:

"Praise God Josephine is going home! I'm happy for her, but I surely will miss her. I've always admired her strength and spirit, and in a sense I've always looked up

to her so much. I don't think she realizes all she's meant to me here or how much I'll miss her."

~

"While here I have never neglected my education. I received my GED and Mom paid for my college education because I wasn't eligible for the grants. So I went to Urbana University where I received credits in their Social Service program and I later attended under the business program they offered. For 18 months I studied as a plumber's apprentice then 18 months as an electrician's apprentice…I studied to be an aerobics instructor and for the past three years I have donated my time to the General Population as well as the Residential Treatment Unit instructing 3 to 4 work outs a week… For the past five years I have studied and mastered the Spanish language. I have been used as an interpreter. My career goal is to study communications and Spanish language at a university level and minor in Iberian history with a focus on Castellano culture. I love Spain.

~

I would like to research how the Spanish Civil War atrocities were over shadowed by the events of WWII… for me the topic to research is how a society can so quickly be so convinced of an ideal on a grand and individual scale that they kill their friends, family and even children for having different beliefs!"

~

"History is so vital to us as human beings. Without history we are doomed to such darkness, such mediocrity, when just a little light shed on the past fosters so much

*growth. Look how my family can stay so stagnant be-
cause it refused to face the past. Now that we are looking
at it there is so much growth. Why do we always fear the
past…once it's past it can no longer attack you."*

~

*"Thank you for the Times article about the "hidden"
Renaissance art. How fascinating! In pictures I see I
am left speechless by the scale of some of those works.
Really it is the work of genius. For a human to cap-
ture a human feeling and give it visual proportion is
AMAZING to me. I could stare for hours at Velazquez
Las Meninas. To most eyes it's just a spoiled little girl,
but to me it demonstrates how all little girls feel before
the pain of life touches them…and the King and Queen
shown as reflections, for me, is the way we often long for
that innocence."*

~

Many of the women I corresponded with had tragic his-
tories of abusive childhoods, as Vanessa did. It was a common
pattern. One woman's story stood out for its brutality; she
had been horribly abused by her parents. She didn't write me
often, but I'll never forget her letters. The first letter was almost
illegible, with writing scrawled across the pages horizontally,
vertically and diagonally, and tiny printing around the edges
of the pages. The only part I could make out was that she was
now medication free. Over time, her letters became progres-
sively more coherent although she was clearly struggling with
very serious mental illness. I always think how different her life
might have been had her childhood been different. Whenever
she wrote to me, I always wrote back. I felt it was critical that
she know someone was there for her, no matter what.

Through my correspondence with the women I learned that many of them had gotten bad advice from their lawyers. In many instances the lawyer advised them not to mention the repeated abuse they suffered. As one woman wrote,

> *"As far as there not being much on domestic violence in my trial goes, my original lawyer was adamant about not having any of the violence brought out, and actually coached me and my son as to what to say during trial to avoid (what happened that evening) being brought out. ...As frightened as I was, I went right along with all he advised, and I concealed as much of what went on—as far as him and me in the bedroom alone—as I could."*

In 1991, one woman I corresponded with applied for clemency under Governor Celeste. Although she had a very strong case, she was not granted clemency in the period before Celeste left office, and her case got bogged down in the new administration. She waited seventeen years to gain her release, and she never gave up hope. Here is one letter she wrote to me:

> *"As you know the 30 of us who were waiting to return to the Parole Board for our clemency's were all suddenly sent denial letters. The new Governor's hands off policy on the issue became painfully evident that dark day in April. I do hear that the Lt. Governor has an open ear to the issue of battered women and that's encouraging to me. It's another 3AM night wondering what God has in mind for the rest of my life, and praying it isn't this*

empty existence here. Now all this clemency business has me real confused. I'm one of the group who has to be returned to the board for additional information. My head is spinning with questions no one can answer."

~

Some who were granted clemency and were preparing to be released expressed their complicated emotions:

"I know you have been contacted about the granting of my clemency. My mother told me of your card and phone conversation. Thank you for caring and taking the time to visit here faithfully... I really want to go to _____ House just for a slow release to society. It's been 7 ½ years since I have functioned in a community. So at times the thoughts are overwhelming. Even tho' I am so ready to greet every opportunity and be a success!! I'm sure we'll see each other before I leave and thank you for your part in my clemency. God involved so many people on this clemency and each part was very instrumental to my freedom."

~

I'm moved that they always ask me how I am, no matter how awful of a time they may be having. And they always express their appreciation for my friendship and correspondence.

"It is always a pleasure to write to you with the knowledge my words are actually considered worthwhile."

~

"I pray that all has settled down for you these days. You remain in my thoughts and prayers always. You give me hope and that alone is a blessing to me."

~

"I was so relieved when I got your letter. The stress of all of this is unbelievable, but I'm hanging in there only through the grace of God"

~

"I thank you for being patient with me and do so appreciate your support Sammy. You're one constant I know I can always count on and that means a lot."

~

"The birthday wishes were most special. Thanks for thinking of me on my special day and keeping me and all the others in your prayers. You all are so good to us."

~

The rules about letter writing to inmates have changed quite a bit over the years in an effort to control the inflow of contraband materials. Volunteers are no longer allowed to write letters, but we are allowed to send birthday cards to L.I.F.E. Group members. The women are given a photocopy of the card, not the actual card. Some women have told me it's the first time they've ever received a birthday card. I'm happy to comply with the rules if it means giving them that one gift. But I do wish I could continue to write letters to them.

Recently, Josephine (who was released in 1991) and I were talking about the L.I.F.E. Group and she told me, "Everyone's joy was getting a letter from Sammy Dyer." That may be the nicest thing anyone has ever said to me. I'm happy that I could give the women a boost by having a connection with the outside world. But I'm happiest that my "sisters" and I were able to share our thoughts and feelings, and get to know each other through our letters.

Chapter Nine

Lives Redeemed

Not long before I started volunteering at the shelter in 1978, a movement began in Ohio that would ultimately lead to clemency being granted to a select group of battered women who were incarcerated for killing their batterers. Statistics on rates of incarceration relating to domestic violence weren't available in the 1970's, but by 2016 it was estimated that 80 to 85 percent of women imprisoned in the United States attributed their incarceration to their association with a batterer, either because they were forced to participate in the crime, or because the crime was directly related to the abuser.[3] I learned this first hand when I began volunteering with the L.I.F.E. Group and met many women who were in prison for defending themselves against their batterer.

---

[3] Schornstein, Jackie. Lessons from the Past: Revitalizing the Clemency Movement for Battered Women Incarcerated for Killing Their Abuser.. Women Leading Change: Case Studies on Women, Gender, and Feminism, [S.l.], v. 1, n. 1, jul. 2016. Available at: http://journals.tulane.edu/index.php/ncs/article/view/1094/998. Date accessed: 19 Jan. 2019.

In the 1970's and 80's we were fortunate in Ohio to have Richard Celeste, first as Lieutenant Governor and then Governor. He and his wife Dagmar were committed to addressing the issue of domestic violence. They did a great deal to raise awareness, from opening their Cleveland home in the mid-1970's as a shelter for battered women to creating a Task Force on Family Violence. The advocates at the shelter were involved in these and other efforts to raise awareness. Although I had only been volunteering for a short time, the advocates included me in many discussions, sharing as much information as was available. There wasn't much in the news about this growing movement in those early days and I felt like I had the inside scoop.

As part of Dagmar Celeste's work with the Task Force, she visited the Ohio Reformatory for Women. She learned that many of the women had been victims of domestic violence and were serving long sentences, often life sentences, for killing their abusers. In spite of her efforts to raise awareness and bring about change, progress was slow in Ohio. Even in the late 1980's, Ohio was one of the few remaining states that did not recognize and allow the battered woman syndrome[4] as a legal defense.

Progress was jump-started in 1990 by Ohio State House Representative Joseph Koziura's introduction of Ohio House Bill 484 which established the battered woman syndrome as a legitimate legal defense that could be used in Ohio courts. In 1988 Representative Koziura heard a program on the radio featuring Dr. Lenora Walker—a psychologist, founder of the

[4] The battered woman syndrome is defined as "the highly variable symptom complex of physical and psychological injuries exhibited by a woman repeatedly abused especially physically by her mate." (Merriam Webster's Dictionary) https://www.merriam-webster.com/dictionary/batteredwomansyndrome
Date accessed: January 19, 2019

Domestic Violence Institute, and developer of the theory of the battered woman syndrome. During the program Dr. Walker named the states that had yet to adopt legislation recognizing the battered woman syndrome as a viable defense and allowing expert testimony proving a woman suffered from the syndrome. When Representative Koziura heard that Ohio was one of them, he decided it was time for a change. He researched the existing legislation and opinions from other states and began drafting what would become Ohio House Bill 484, now codified as Ohio Revised Code §2901.06.

Joe Clark, (Brother Joe of the L.I.F.E. Group), remembers when Representative Kozuira visited the Ohio Reformatory for Women in Marysville and interviewed many women incarcerated for having killed, or paid someone to kill, their batterer. Mr. Kozuira was struck by the length of sentences these women received relative to sentences given to men for equivalent crimes. This made no sense to him, fueling his resolve to get the bill passed. Joe Clark was impressed with Mr. Koziura's sincerity, and his empathy for the women. "He was one of the good guys," Joe said.

There was quite a bit of opposition to the bill, but Mr. Koziura persisted with the strong support of Governor Richard Celeste, Lieutenant Governor Lee Fisher, Jane Campbell (who later became Cleveland's first female mayor) and many others. His bill was signed into law on August 6, 1990. Passage of this bill was a huge step forward and it paved the way for Governor Celeste, with the support of his wife Dagmar, to set a clemency process in motion that was unparalleled in Ohio or anywhere in the country. The Governor reviewed over 100 cases of women incarcerated for killing or assaulting a batterer, ultimately commuting the sentences of 25 women. In these cases he found the women had received overly severe sentences given the horrific abuse they endured, evidence of which would have shown they acted in self-defense and suffered from the battered woman syndrome, had it been presented during their trials.

Becky Cardine, the case manager at ORW, was assigned the task of selecting cases for the Governor and his team to review. With the help of Joe Clark, Becky organized focus groups with women who were victims of domestic violence. I was visiting Vanessa regularly at ORW at that time, and this was when Joe Clark contacted me to ask if I would be willing to help facilitate the focus groups, given my experience in the shelter.

The clemency applications were lengthy, and with over 100 cases identified and a tight time frame to get them to the State Parole Board, Becky put the L.I.F.E Group members to work typing the applications. In preparing the applications, as the New York Times reported, "(t)he women produced emergency room records documenting bruises and broken bones, brought in police reports and doctor's statements and in some cases had witnesses testify to the abuse."[5] By working hard to meet the deadline, over 100 women were given a chance to go before the State Parole Board to present evidence of past abuse. After having been denied the chance to relate the details of their abuse at their trial, these women finally had a chance to tell their story and be heard. It was a watershed moment for domestic violence awareness both here in Ohio and nationally. Everyone at the shelter was thrilled with this huge step forward.

Governor Celeste and Joe Kozuira made history with Ohio House Bill 484 and the commutation of the sentences of 25 women imprisoned for saving their own lives.

One of those women was my friend Josephine Adkins.

---

[5] Wilkerson, Isabel, *Clemency Granted to 25 Women Convicted for Assault or Murder*, N.Y. Times, Dec. 22, 1990.

Chapter Ten

Josephine

Of all the people I've met in my 41 years volunteering with battered women, Josephine Adkins stands out. She is one of the strongest, bravest, most intelligent and inspirational people I've ever known. Josephine's story is both heartbreaking and encouraging.

Our paths crossed a few times in the early years of my involvement at the shelter, and then as the years went on we saw each other regularly, becoming close friends and colleagues. When Joe called me in 1990 to ask if I would be interested in going to ORW with him to talk to the L.I.F.E. Group, he told me an interesting story of how he started going to the L.I.F.E. Group meetings, having to do with Josephine:

"I was running a tutoring group at the St. Martin de Porres Family Center affiliated with my church. The group was made up of kids from the projects in the Glenville area in Cleveland. One morning I learned that the father of two of our students had been shot and killed. When I got to the church that afternoon a very young, sweet, fully-veiled and very religious nun came to the door.

I asked if she had heard that the two students' father had been shot and killed the night before. I'll never forget how she looked off into space and serenely said "Well, that's not all bad."

"Whoa," I thought. I wanted to know more about this family. I found out about six months later that Josephine, the girls' mother, had been arrested for the murder. Because her children were in the tutoring program, I kept in touch with her. She asked me to be a sort of spiritual advisor to her. I was able to get to see her in the county jail quite often, and I followed her through the trial. It was never clear to me exactly who did it, but she apparently paid someone to kill her husband.

During the trial, it became obvious that her husband was not a very nice man. I started to understand what the nun at the school meant about his death not being all that bad. I gradually learned that from 1968 until his death Josephine's husband brought down a continuous reign of terror on the family. He threatened to shoot their oldest boy during an argument about his dog, actually shooting into the floor right next to his foot. He had an affair with a friend of Josephine's who was living in the house with them. He beat and abused Josephine on many occasions over eighteen years. In 1974 he held Josephine in their apartment for an entire week, during which time she was beaten almost continuously. Finally, she was able to call her mother on the telephone and tell her about the situation. Her mother called the police who took Josephine to Metro Hospital for treatment. In the emergency room her mother walked past Josephine without even recognizing her because she was so badly beaten.

In February of 1985, he beat Josephine with an iron and a wooden slat. She still carries the scars on her face after once again being beaten beyond recognition. The incidents of abuse against Josephine were too numerous to count. When Josephine found out that he was also regularly sexually molesting their oldest daughter, well, that just sent her over the edge.

She was sentenced to 23 years to life at the Ohio Reformatory for Women in Marysville, Ohio, three hours away. I continued to visit her there, and brought her kids to see her as much as possible. My official title at the parish at that time was Director of the Neighborhood Center, so all of this was just part of my job.

Josephine managed her time in prison well from the start. She was encouraged to join the newly formed L.I.F.E. Group. She then became the second president of the group. Soon, she wrote to me and asked if I would come and give an inspirational talk to the group. I gave the talk, and it was terrible! I did not connect with the group, for two reasons. One was that I had no idea about prison life. The other was that I was the wrong gender and had the wrong background. So, I asked if I could come back the next month and bring someone else. I asked another parishioner of mine, Frances, if she would like to give a talk to the L.I.F.E. Group and she consented. The two of us went the next month and she began her talk with the statement, "I could be here."

Frances described her life in Detroit as a battered spouse, and how she decided to leave with her children. Sitting at the kitchen table with a butcher knife after yet another beating she knew she had a choice; either kill her husband and lose everything, or try to leave and save herself and her children. She gathered the children in the middle of the night and went to the bus station in downtown Detroit and took the first bus out. It brought them to Cleveland, where she started a new life.

The women were spellbound by her talk. That is how we got started, and Frances and I kept going every month. We picked up another regular volunteer, Willa. And we three have been going ever since."

As Joe finished telling me his story I realized that I had met Josephine a few years earlier when she was at the Women Together shelter. I told Joe I had actually picked her up when she came in to shelter with her three younger children. She didn't stay long, but I remembered her well. I was sorry to hear about what had happened to her. I was grateful to Joe for all he had done for her.

I became very close to Josephine through my visits to the L.I.F.E. Group, and her story captivated me. She has given me permission to share her story, in the hopes that it might help someone else. I'll let her tell it in her own words:

"The breaking point for me was the sexual abuse of my daughter. I found out in 1983, when she was about 18. I will never forget that day. It was like all the abuse I'd suffered for all the years came together in one moment that changed me forever.

My husband had moved back in after being apart from us for about a year. I let him come stay with us because, well the children, you know they loved their father. He was probably going to get put out of the big apartment we had in the projects because they had found out we weren't there anymore. We were in a big house then, and the boys said "Mom, why don't you let him come stay with us." I said okay, because...you know I would cry sometimes because I wanted my children to be with their father until the end. I had mine, and a lot of my upbringing was traditional with my father in the house and my mother a stay at home mom until we were teenagers. And, well, I guess I thought maybe it would stop. My father was abusive to my mother, but only when they were drinking, and not severe, never like that. When they didn't drink it stopped. He never hit us, my mother was the strong hand, and it kind of stopped after we were all teenagers. So I thought maybe this would stop.

We were good for about six months. For those first six months he was back we had no relationship. Then he decided there should be a relationship between us and the abuse started again. Incidents were fewer in number but more severe. Much more severe.

The day that I found out what he did to my daughter, me and her were sitting on the porch, no one else home. I was sitting and she was standing and she said "I know you don't like him, I don't like him either, but I will tell you something that will make you hate him." I looked up at her and said "Don't say another word, I know what you're going to say. I'm going to my bedroom and I'm going to stay there awhile. When I come down I'll be okay." I had not let myself acknowledge what he had done to her.

When I came down, I almost think I was a different person. I could not believe I could let that pass. I always felt that mothers are the protectors of their children. How would I be a good mother if I allowed him to be on this earth having done that to my daughter?

After that I think everybody felt there was something different about me. I had made that decision in my head like "he is not gonna be around." If I had a conversation with him, I would think to myself "You won't be around forever you know, you're not gonna be here because this is going to end."

I went and bought a gun and thought, "Okay, now how am I gonna get this done?" I started to plan in my head. What I know now is that my thoughts about having him dead was a result of the trauma and manipulation I experienced from him over 18 years. I made everybody think I was okay, even though I wasn't. I went through this for about six months. I would flash back to scenes in the house when his abuse of my daughter was going down; red flags where I just said to myself "no, that doesn't mean anything." Her in her robe with nothing on underneath when I came back from my night school classes at Cuyahoga Community College (Tri-C); her with her two sisters pulled close to her, all three sleeping in the same bed; or her by herself in the bed with the covers pulled up tight—all red flags. I went through this for about six months, thinking to myself "how could I let him live when he's done something like this to his own child."

I had this vision of him never being around and how my life was gonna take off, how it was gonna be good. I was gonna have fun, and me and the kids could enjoy everything without him. There were so many things I wanted to do and he would always say I was too stupid. I would think how life would be so much different, so much better, if he weren't there. You know I had dealt with that abuse for so long. I had known him since I was fourteen, and married him when I was eighteen. We were married for 20 years and eighteen of them were abusive. I had always thought about getting out. I had been to shelter, but shelter didn't work for me because I wanted to be home, with my children. I had a job too, and night classes for my degree. When I was in shelter I couldn't work or go to my night classes.

That's when I first met Sammy, one time when I tried going to shelter; I don't remember the date now. She picked me and my three younger kids up. I remember she had a station wagon and she picked us up at the Burger King on the corner in the evening. My older daughter was with my husband's mother, and my two older boys stayed with him, so they could do whatever they wanted. The little ones were 7, 9 and 10, with the two girls being the older ones. There were like two sets of kids, the three older and the three younger, because we were apart for some time in between sets. Sammy probably filled out my intake card, she did a little bit of everything back then. We would meet again later at ORW, but that was where it started between me and Sammy. I remembered her after I left; she was definitely one of the good ones.

I could go to my mother's house sometimes to get away from him. I would take the kids there. But he would always be around there, watching. I had tolerated that abuse for so long and the year when we went back together the incidents became very, very severe. It just wasn't going to stop, and I couldn't get away.

For a long time, I found that if I could keep myself busy enough it was like I didn't notice it. I could be at work or at school and that was an escape. I had a job as a teacher at a Head Start school that I got when my daughter was in nursery school. I was a parent volunteer and did all the volunteer things I could. I was there so much they asked me to step in when the teacher went on maternity leave. She never came back so they offered me the job and I took it. I worked there for sixteen years. I was the sole bread winner for my family. I don't know how I did it on those salaries back then. But that's when I got my Associates degree at Tri-C. The program paid for it, and it took me about seven years because I could only go at night part-time.

There was a lot of abuse going on during that time too. I was dealing with that, having and raising six children, just living this kind of rat race every day, but keeping busy, trying to improve myself. He was one of those men where everybody eats dinner together, no play time for the kids until after he had his dinner. I lived by the crock pot, dinner as soon as I got home from work, kids out to play, me in my seat at school by 6pm with one of the kids having rode the bus with me. Home by 8pm to bath and put the kids to bed, always picking up the rooms, toys, laundry as I went, prepare the meal for the next day in the crock pot. Sit down and do my homework until about two or three in the morning. So tired by the end that I would go right to sleep for a few hours, especially if I knew a beat down wasn't coming. I learned how to read the warning signs so I knew if something was going to explode. I usually knew in the morning if it was going to be a physical day or a verbal day. Usually if nothing blew up by the time I went to bed it was over for that day. Getting up before the rest of the house to do two loads of laundry, darks and whites. All the time that house was controlled by his domestic violence. I was fine as long as I was busy. Until that didn't work anymore.

I now know there was one time I tried to kill myself. That was when we lived in the projects on the third floor. He had started his stuff and I ran in the bathroom and locked the door. He yelled from outside the door "If you don't come out of this bathroom I'm gonna kick the door in and I'm gonna kill you – I'm gonna kill you." He would choke me until I passed out, wake me up and choke me again until I passed out again. When you're passing out, it's like going through twilight; it's almost like you're dead. So I knew he would do it, and I knew what it would feel like. I still don't know how I did it but when I saw that door coming down I climbed out that little window and hung there in my bare feet and night gown and just dropped. A tree broke my fall a little bit so I survived but I did break my leg. I crawled around the building to get away and there he was. He picked me up and took me to the hospital; told them I fell. When we left he asked me if I wanted to go home or to my mother's house. I told him my mother's house and he said okay. But then he took me home instead. I had no choice.

Then this thing with my daughter, her leaving the house along with my older boys. The boys would say "We gotta go Mom, because you and Dad just keep fighting. We wish you all would stop and we love you both, so we just have to leave now." I remember thinking to myself "I'm losing all the pieces I really want." I didn't want him anymore and he always swore one day he was gonna kill me, kill the kids or kill himself. That's what kept me from leaving. And made me afraid to stay. I didn't want to die that way and I didn't want my children to die that way. He always had a gun laying around and when he would lock that door at night, I was terrified. He always did his abuse at night. During the day he could be happy, but at night he would pick it up and he'd start: "I should take this gun – I'll blow your brains out."

He did shoot at me in the house at times. I was afraid that if I left and stayed away he would find me and I would end up dead somewhere, either in the house or out on the street somewhere. A lot of times I would look up and turn around and there he was. That's fear within itself.

I felt he was very capable of killing any one of us, including himself. I didn't really know it back then but he had some very real mental health issues and would have bouts where he would talk about his childhood with me at night. We would spend hours talking about it. He had a horrible childhood. He loved his mother, but he didn't like her. There was domestic violence in the house and she left, leaving him with his father. His father married another woman who didn't like him and treated him very badly. What I know about mental health now makes me understand he had some very serious mental health problems. I think he resented my relationship with my children. I think he was very jealous of the bonding I had with them.

On top of what he did to my daughter, he was physically abusive to the children, and very controlling. He controlled everything in the house, made all the decisions. I would try to help the kids out, stepping up to say something when he would punish them. He would say "If you don't shut up and sit down you're going to get some too." Sometimes it was so severe with the kids I would step up mid-way to take the beat down for them. It was just a house of turmoil. To be afraid to live in your own house, afraid when the door gets shut, dragging your kids out in the middle of the night trying to get away; that's no kind of life. In the end I just had to sacrifice myself and save my kids. My oldest boy had told me if he beat me one more time he would kill him. I couldn't let that happen, couldn't let him ruin his life that way.

My middle daughter always came to my defense. No matter what was going on she stepped up. Even when she was little she'd run and grab me and hold on and cry and beg "Dad, please leave my Mommy alone, please don't hit her no more." When he punished them he would hit her more severe than the others. The girls shared rooms and would be each other's protectors; they would get in bed together, hug each other and say "don't cry, don't cry." I know he sexually abused my oldest daughter, and I will always wonder if anything happened with the others, but they always said no. One of the girls was always very nervous and had a learning disability at school. When he died all that went away.

I had already talked to somebody that I knew, a very close friend, about how I wish my husband would die, that he was dead…and the picture unfolded. I told my friend I had to do something. I never thought it would come to light like what really happened in the end but it did. I didn't even know it had been done. I just knew his car was out on the street one morning and he was in it, shot dead.

I plead not guilty, and the story that unfolded in court was not how it happened, even though the people telling the story were the ones who actually played out the part with me. My husband's family was there and denied all the abuse and the part with my daughter. I knew they knew about that, because my daughter told me that's why they wanted her to live with them; so they could keep the secret close to home.

I believed the court would see that something wasn't right, but they didn't, and I got the guilty verdict. That was the only time I cried about it. Because I lost my chance to raise my younger children without the badness. I had to go away and by the time I came back they were older and into their own trouble.

I was in the county jail for a year before going to court. Spend a year in a county jail and you agree to anything to get out of there. Nothing to do, not one bit of privacy; you just sit all day, waiting for the next day. You finally just say "whatever it is just give it to me" and you agree to any sentence just to go someplace else. It might be better.

But I didn't have any regrets about what happened, and I never punished myself about it. It seemed like my world had crumbled, but I was fine. I had kind of set my children free. And I was free, even though I had to go stay at Marysville (ORW).

After he died we had about a year together, me and my children, before it starting falling down. During that year I did my own therapy. I promised I would never marry again or put another man in my house, because I couldn't deal with that. I talked to my children about their father. I told them "you should love him because that's your Dad." We had pictures of him in the house and I never took that away from them because that was their father.

When they found out what really happened at first they said "No, no, no, my mother had no part of that." In the end I kept saying "Yes, I did." They said "How? You loved my father." I explained love have nothing to with it; it was just protection of the family. I kept my promise and did not marry or have another relationship. I had to become the flip side of who I was, and that's exactly what happened. We were free. We were able to do a lot of stuff together. And we enjoyed it. That was a good year.

So even when I went to Marysville I had no regrets. I knew that bad part of my life was over. My family was free from worrying about when the next incident would happen. My children were placed where they could be okay with my mother and my sister. Even my mother was okay. She did not like it that I had to go away but she was fine. I wasn't worried when I went in because I knew that by the grace of God I wasn't gonna be there long. I knew something was gonna happen. After about eight years it did.

I got to see my children while I was in Marysville, thanks to Brother Joe Clark. He knew them all from the community school where he worked. He would bring them to see me and kept track of them as best he could during that time. The older boys were out of school, and the younger got moved out of the community school due to difficulties he was having. Joe would always check on my oldest daughter and the two younger ones at the community school. He helped them get some tuition money from the community school for Erie View Catholic. He did as much as he could.

My life really changed when I went to Marysville. I told myself just to find something to be busy. I became more outgoing and friendly to people, more helpful. In Marysville, if you don't do that you're gonna sink into nothing. I had felt like I was a people person before, but could never be that way because of him. I think I always knew how to step outside myself and look at myself and situations to figure things out. I did that a lot in Marysville. Often at night I would look out my window, step outside myself and go visit my family and friends in my mind. By morning I would come back, ready for another day. It was a good way to get through the nights.

Ms. Cardine was the case manager at that time, and she was very good at reading files and identifying people who should not be there. I think I was one of them, because I ended up with a very nice job there in private industry, not working for the institution. I made mops at that job. Not so interesting but a decent job with decent pay. I was so fortunate to have met someone who understood what had happened and kept placing me where I was comfortable. She got me involved in the L.I.F.E. Group. That was a group of women who were really looked up to, and I guess she thought I was one, or could be. I was able to laugh and talk with these women who had been there for a very long time and learn how they did it, how they stayed okay. I learned from them. I did become one who was looked up to. I was the second elected President of the L.I.F.E Group Executive Committee Board.

That's when I ran into Sammy again. Brother Joe Clark was involved with the group after I asked him to come speak, and he reached out to her. He was trying to help Ms. Cardine organize discussion groups to discuss battered women's issues and to help some women get clemency, and somehow he got Sammy involved. I knew that would be a good thing when she got into that group. She started coming every month and would bring Frances, who Joe had gotten started coming in, and Willa, who had been incarcerated there. Willa, in her own words, came to "give back to the sisterhood." She worked at a shelter for a while after she got out, and she was involved with the clemency package process. She sent women who were victims of domestic violence questionnaires to complete to determine if they were eligible for clemency or parole based on the battered woman syndrome. Willa stayed with the L.I.F.E. Group even after she got fired from the shelter. Something about 4th of July fireworks she set off so the kids could have some fun. She was kind of a firecracker herself.

I had served almost eight years of my sentence when Ms. Cardine and Brother Joe got me into the clemency application program. Brother Joe wrote the letter of support for my application. He and Ms. Cardine helped me with that application. Thanks to both of them I was very fortunate to be granted clemency by Governor Celeste. It really helped to have people like Ms. Cardine, Mr. Joseph Koziura, Joe Clark and Sammy Dyer on my side. I had every intention of dedicating myself to helping other victims of domestic violence when I got out of Marysville, and I did. When my clemency was granted, part of the package was that I had to do 200 hours of community service at a domestic violence shelter. I got out in April 1991, and by June I was working at the Domestic Violence (DV) Center.

A bit later, I think it was Sammy that told me about the job opening at Templum House. So I went and applied and got hired. At that time shelters were looking for women who knew domestic violence, and that for sure was me. The staff at the shelter taught me so much. I knew what I had been through, but I hadn't known all the words for it all. I didn't know all the psychology behind domestic violence. They taught me all that. I became the one who always did all the domestic violence group sessions in the shelter, because I was able to understand and really know what the women were saying because I had lived it. I would share pieces of my story, not the bad end because I didn't ever want a woman to think that was the path to take, but some of the beatings, scenes from the house and some of the things he would say, and what he would do. I would just let the women talk and I knew in my gut what they said was the truth, because it had happened to me. I learned to staff the hotline really well too. I had very good training. I mean very good training.

They even taught me how to drive a car. Almost 40 years old and I didn't even know how to drive a car. I really didn't know anything. I had to learn how to drive because everybody working at the shelter had to be able to do pick-ups and drop offs. My brothers and sisters thought this was a joke because I never drove, and my brothers would not help me learn to drive. They said "What are you talking about, you need this for your job? We'll believe it when we see it." So my co-workers taught me to drive. When I became a driver my brothers said "We can't believe this, you driving a car." But they were happy for me.

Sammy was at the East side shelter at that time, and Templum was on the West side so we didn't work at shelter together, but we did get together not too long after I was granted clemency. There was a conference on domestic violence in Chicago; I think it was called the 6th Round Table Conference in Defense of Battered Women; something like that. Sammy, Willa, Frances and Joe were all going, and Templum agreed that I should go as part of my training. There were some rules for me about crossing state lines relating to my clemency. I had to make sure I had all my paperwork—work and court permissions—together because I had to check in at the police station near the conference in Chicago. It was like parole, only more lenient because I could leave the state of Ohio. But if I failed to check in where I was supposed to be that would be a problem.

So me, Sammy, Willa and Frances drove to Chicago together, just the girls. I had never done anything like this and I enjoyed every minute. We got to the police station where I needed to check in and we all went in. I was nervous but had my three friends standing there supporting me so I was okay. The police officer took all kinds of time looking through my paper work, like he was trying to find some reason not to let me go on to the conference. Sammy told me later she thought it was because I was black. I don't know if it was that, or because I was a woman and maybe he knew what happened. Maybe he was a batterer himself. I don't know.

After a while Sammy got kind of tired of the whole thing and stepped up and asked him very respectfully what the problem was. He looked at her and said, not so respectfully "And who are you?" Well, Sammy pulled herself up really tall (and she was already pretty tall), looked down on him and said "Well, I'm Mrs. John J. Dyer, Jr.!" And he sort of looked down, shuffled some papers and stammered out, "Then I guess everything seems okay here. She can go on."

We three were just staring at Sammy, and straight faced she thanked him. She turned around and held her arms out for us saying "Let's go then." We all linked arms and we could see her straight face turning to a smile but she kept whispering "Don't laugh, don't laugh," while we walked out of the building. As soon as we got outside and some steps away from the door we all just fell out laughing so hard, Sammy most of all! We all kept saying, "Who are you?" "Well, I'm Mrs. John J. Dyer, Jr.!" and laughing so hard. She took my fear away in that moment, the way she stood up for me with nothing but her own nerve. That's who Sammy is, always willing to stand up for what she knows is right. But we did *tease her about that "Well, I'm Mrs. John J. Dyer, Jr." for a long time. She laughed every time.*

We had a good time at that conference. I learned a lot, met a lot of people working hard on the domestic violence issues. That's also where I figured out there was a good chemistry between Brother Joe Clark and Sister Mary Dwyer. They were there and I could see what was what between them, even though they couldn't at that time. I kept nudging Sammy and trying to tell her, quietly, so they wouldn't be embarrassed. They finally figured it out and got married later on. That was a good thing for them. They had to leave their church orders, but that part was okay. That didn't change who they are and they kept doing good for others no matter where they were.

When I came home from prison I found my children had some mental health issues, and some drugs and domestic violence issues. It made me sad that I had missed the chance to raise them without the badness. It didn't surprise me though, given what they had experienced and witnessed. It would make me so sad when my children would come in and see me all bloody and beat up and suffering. They would cry.

My middle daughter got into drugs and a domestic violence situation. When she would get beat by her boyfriend the little boy next door would call me. I would go over with the police. One time it was one of the policemen who used to come over to my place. He looked at me and said, "You still around?" and I said, "Yeah, you still around?" Then he said, "Is this repeating itself?" and I said, "I hope not."

That time was very bad. Her boyfriend came after her and threw her down to the ground so hard her hand busted through the skin. She stayed in the hospital a couple days. He got locked up. There was a hearing and I called Sammy to do that with her. My daughter was so angry with me it didn't help for me to be at the hearing. Sammy went with her and talked to her and helped her be strong enough to tell what happened. She never would have gotten out of that situation alive if it wasn't for Sammy.

Whatever kind of advice Sammy gave my daughter it sure got passed on to my daughter's kids, even if she didn't always take it herself. My grand-daughters are all good. They are all state licensed Nursing Assistants (STNA's), and they know how to work. They are not involved in domestic violence, they could care less about relationships. When they get a new boyfriend they say "Grandma I'm trying to get my new boyfriend over here to meet you" and I say "I don't really have time to meet your new boyfriend" and they say "I know, but he hears stories about you and he's afraid of you." And I say, "Well, listen it goes like this with me: "Hello, how are you, I am not your friend, I am her Grandmother, so if Grandmother has something to say to you, it won't be your friend that's saying it." They say "Grandma you're so mean!" And I say "No, I'm not. If it's not right, I don't feel bad about saying it's not right." So history has stopped repeating itself for now, anyway.

One of my granddaughters once said "You know you're like a legend around here don't you?" I don't know where that came from but I think everybody in the neighborhood knew about the abuse, because sometimes I ran out of the house, and it ended up outside with the police and all that. So they all knew, and I think a lot of them were afraid of him. I don't know what else he did outside the house. So when he got it, (as they say "he got it") they all said "Wow, she did it. And he used to do her so bad." And then I went off to prison and my children were left behind. And then I came back. So I guess they thought 'She was supposed to have been gone, and now here she is back and she puts all this back together with her children and a house and a job and all this.'

Once I started working, I worked as much as I could at different shelters and with different programs, part time and full time and anytime, keeping busy, helping other women. I started working in 1991 and have worked seven days a week ever since. I never needed much sleep and there was just so much I wanted to do after being set free twice, once from him and once from Marysville. I didn't want to waste any time.

I got to a point where I made pretty good money, especially with all the overtime I worked. A lot better than when I was raising my kids. I enjoyed doing things for my grandchildren, like helping my granddaughter set up her first apartment. She would say "I just love you so much Grandma, you helped me put this house together and bought me all these things for it." I just want them to be okay and not have to struggle. I just try to show them the way a little bit.

I've enjoyed being able to do birthday parties for people. I don't do them for me, though, because I'm blessed every day. There was a time I didn't think I would be here.

I do eat ice cream though, and there's a Mitchell's down the street, so I go there twice a week and bring a pint back to work and sit down and eat it. The girls say "Miss Jo, you are so wrong! Eating that ice cream when you didn't bring us any!" And I say "No, I did not – this is MY treat." And we laugh at that.

Now at age 70, I'm still working two jobs. And I'm still taking classes. There got to be so much drug and alcohol use going on in the shelter where I work that I thought I should get trained in helping people overcome addiction. Somebody needs to know something about all that in the shelter. I already know the domestic violence piece of it. I've taken a lot of the classes to get what's called a Chemical Dependency Counselor Assistant. I'm just a notch away from taking the test to that I can work in a treatment facility.

I'm happy about the whole thing. I have anxieties about leaving my job at the Center for Domestic Violence because I've worked there for 27 years. But I need something to rejuvenate me, to lift me up, because I know domestic violence and I've conquered that piece.

I understand me, and what happened. And I can look back and not feel afraid to look back. And I tell the women a lot of times, when you're able to visit back there and talk about it and not hold it in, then you may be able to help yourself in the near future.

I wrote the following essay, "I Am a Survivor," when I was asked to give a talk about my experiences."

I AM A SURVIVOR

by Josephine Adkins

Being a victim of domestic abuse and a receiver of clemency granted by former Ohio Governor Richard Celeste, I have a lot of feelings and thoughts to share about the stages of violence.

I began my relationship with my former husband when I was 14, resulting in marriage at age 18. That marriage lasted for 20 years, and 18 of those were violence. I can say that the relationship had a dual role of love and hate. I, as a woman, love to be pampered and told how much I am needed, wanted and loved. When the violence in our marriage happened, love always followed. Love became the dominant force built around our relationship. It was easy for me to accept apologies when it was given with tears, promises and so much warmth and care. I do not mind saying at this point that sexual behavior said much to me and that I could forgive the abuser because he meant nothing but love. The ultimate advice from everyone to whom I turned for help was "I would not take that and you should leave." With no advice of the how-to process and support, I placed a lot of emphasis on material thigs such as my home, furniture, clothing and jobs.

So I learned to pick up on the warning signs the abuser gave me and thus I learned I could sometimes avoid a violent situation. Each day when my abuser arose to begin his day, he gave clues as to what kind of day it would be: a day of mental abuse or a day of physical abuse. The clues were ones of body language, eye contact, and general conversation. My abuser was a person who was aggressive, dominant, egotistical, and very macho. He had to also be the leader in anything he did. He was illiterate and tried to hide this fact. He lacked the knowledge of how to have a healthy relationship and the tools to work on a stressful and unwanted problem in the household. He then turned to the use of force in any way he could to control me.

Then I learned that my love for my children complicated my abuser's life. He began to abuse the children to manipulate and control me. Because I was the victim of an abuser I was ashamed, and thus I lied to anyone who questioned me about any bad situation that occurred. So I tended to go about my way, living day to day and thinking how nice life would be if the abuser would live up to his words of love and care.

After having said a lot of things about the abusive ups and downs, one other thing happened to complicate matters. My abusive relationship went on for a long period of time. During that time, I was, for the most part, sole provider for our family. I began to outgrow my abuser, moving up the career ladder and going through a knowledge-seeking process. I began to say to myself, "I like what I am doing, I like who I am, and this matter has to end somewhere." My abuser then became the target of thoughts of removal from the household. Thought was given to removing him from the power and control he held over the children and me.

This is where I began having thoughts of taking his life. I felt it is a thought I should not be having. A person should not intentionally want to take a life. But by the same token, I did *not want to continue to accept the abuse that will put an end to my life. This thought pops into my mind when I was alone, at the most unwanted times. Most definitely it came after a violent attack and surely confirmed what I was thinking. It began to haunt me just like a bad dream and became part of my daily thoughts.*

At the end of my history of domestic violence came my incarceration. Incarceration can be very peaceful, if you choose to let it. One thing for sure, I had peace of mind because my abuser no longer existed. Therefore, I could accept incarceration. I had accepted unwanted situations for years. So I began to plan this wonderful future that I had thought about so often during my abuse, but had to be on hold for a while. I began to look inside myself, finding out who I was, what I was about. I thought about how to practice self-expression, self-control, self-confidence, and how to be assertive. My wants and dislikes became very valuable tools for me to use to protect and guarantee having a promising future. I figured out that the best way to do my time in the institution was to take part in what groups offered, go to school, become supportive of others and have concern for others. Most definitely, I moved about in a positive manner to ensure the institution I was not a threat to it or society.

I also wanted to be respected as a human being and a person who could live outside the institution with no problem, if allowed. My secret of getting through my prison term was this: Late at night, after lock-in time, I would get very busy in my room. I would look out the window, past the gates and would visit my family and friends. I would replay happy events of sharing with family and friends. I would read for basic information, write letters, and make short and long-term goals. I could step outside myself and look at myself to better evaluate something that has happened in a day's time.

After having done all that, I would return to the institution in the morning. I stayed out of crowds that were a threat to my positive stay in the institution. One thing I know for sure, prison does not rehabilitate you. You have to do that yourself! Being a person who had a very good reason to do what I did, I rehabilitated myself after it happened. I know the key to it all now: I am a human being. I do not want my wants, needs, and feelings shoved aside where I cannot feel any self-worth, pride or respect.

I am very grateful and appreciative for what was given to me by Governor Celeste and somewhere, I think I was in the hands of God because I still have my life. My future holds concern, great respect, admiration and understanding for others who are victims of domestic violence and are incarcerated because of it. I have promised myself I will always find the time to lend a helping hand, a listening ear and a shoulder to cry on. I can very well relate to their situation of violence. I am a survivor!

Chapter Eleven

Resilience and Strength

As I look back over my 41 years of volunteering with battered women, I have to smile to myself at the naïve woman I was when I first picked up the phone to call the shelter and ask about volunteering. There was so much I didn't know! This experience has truly been a journey of discovery—both about the issue of domestic violence and about myself. It has also been a journey of love. Love given to and received from the staff advocates at the shelter, from the victims, and from the women in the L.I.F.E. Group.

While I have focused my work on the personal side of the issue of domestic violence, I am also aware of the political reality in which battered women live. I feel the issue of domestic violence still does not get the attention it deserves in our country to truly break the cycle of abuse. An estimated six million women in the U.S. are physically abused each year,[6] and an estimated 4,500 women in the U.S. are incarcerated

[6] National Coalition Against Domestic Violence: Statistics https://ncadv.org/statistics

for defending their lives or the lives of their children against batterers.[7] There is a dire need for more shelters, more advocacy, and for legislation to protect victims. I frequently hear stories in the news of women who have gotten out of abusive relationships only to be later murdered by their abuser. Often the abuser had not been held or charged during previous incidents of abuse, ignoring the danger they pose. A recent tragic case right here in Shaker Heights was that of Aisha Fraser, a young Shaker Heights School District teacher who was murdered by her abusive ex-husband four years after she divorced him following a brutal beating.

Former Ohio Governor Dick Celeste, his wife Dagmar Celeste, and former State Representative Joe Kozuira did so much to help victims of domestic violence, setting an example for other elected officials. I'm encouraged that other politicians are following in their footsteps. Slowly we are seeing progress in Ohio. In 2018 Ohio passed legislation that provides stricter penalties for domestic violence charges, disallows plea bargains in domestic violence cases, enacts tougher gun restrictions for those convicted of domestic assault, and expands these laws to include dating violence. Legislation has been proposed for the 2019-2020 session that would make choking and strangulation felonies rather than misdemeanors, in addition to further tightening up loopholes and enforcing stricter penalties for incidents of domestic violence. Should this legislation pass, Ohio would become the 43rd state to enact felony choking and strangulation laws. Another

---

National Center for Disease Control "The National Intimate Partner and Sexual Violence Survey 2010" https://www.cdc.gov/violenceprevention/pdf/nisvs_report2010-a.pdf

[7] The Ohio Justice and Policy Center, the Women's Project
http://www.ohiojpc.org/what-we-do/legal-services/womens-project/

important proposal currently pending in the Ohio legislature is Aisha's Law, proposed in honor of Aisha Fraser. Aisha's Law is geared toward screening reports of domestic violence to identify high risk cases and provide support and services for the victim. These are all positive forward steps, yet there is much work left to do. (See Appendix for resources and ways to help.)

I feel grateful for the opportunity I have had to get to know and sit beside the brave women I met at the shelter and at ORW. From the beginning I felt a strong connection to these women, and I've wanted to help in any way I can. I want them to know that they're loved, respected, and valued.

I tried to practice what my father preached—not judging someone whose shoes I have not walked in. Hearing these women's heart-breaking stories opened my eyes beyond the idyllic childhood I'd had. I tried my best to quietly listen, not showing any shock or emotion, aiming to emulate the caring manner of the advocates at the Women Together shelter. While I listened to the stories of these women, I felt my compassion expanding. Though I did not walk in their shoes, I tried to journey beside them as a faithful friend.

This work was hard at times, but I never thought about not going or giving up. Progress could seem slow or nonexistent at times, but then a woman would say or do something that would indicate that she was taking a step forward and it would encourage me to carry on. The strength and courage of these women gives me continuing hope in the possibility of growth and healing.

Many times, I was in tears driving home from the L.I.F.E. Group meetings at ORW. I remember one night driving home by myself. I started thinking about the women in the L.I.F.E. Group and all the things they had accomplished— the gospel choir, the writing of plays and short stories, the fundraising and donating to charities. How each of them has something special that is unique to them, some kind of gift. All I could think about was my Dad saying, "Everybody has something special about them. No matter where they live, or how much money they have." As I was thinking this, suddenly the moon broke through a series of clouds. In that moment I understood my father's words more clearly than ever before. *Everybody has something special about them.* I felt a powerful connection with my father, and I became overwhelmed with gratitude as I realized the women at the shelter and at ORW had enabled me to see the true depth of his words.

Other times driving home I would go over a conversation in my head that I had had with a woman. I would be so furious that she had been so damaged as a little child, wondering how anybody could neglect and hurt a child so badly. I would get very angry, and question what is wrong with our society that so many people suffer so much. I didn't let the women know that their stories made me cry, but I did tell them that what happened to them made me angry. I never hesitated to tell them that the abuse they suffered was wrong.

As they told me about their childhoods, I understood what would lead them to make the decisions that they made, such as to run off with a drug dealer at age 15, or stay with an abuser.

Becky Cardine, the former case manager at ORW and founder of the L.I.F.E. Group, wrote movingly about the ways society has let these women down in a letter to Joe Clark. She wrote:

"Many of our members have committed heinous crimes and society feels that they deserve nothing better but to vegetate in prison. However,... I have discovered that the very society who rejects this individual was very often the one who created her. She was hungry, she needed clothes, she needed a caring person who would not abuse or betray her, and not even her most basic needs were met. Society rages against the child abuser! Everyone rushes to condemn this individual but not enough effort is expended to treat the child. Then when this child turns 18, all of a sudden she doesn't deserve our concern or protection. A prison cell is good enough for what all the clamoring about the poor victim of child abuse was about only a few years before."

I felt this same anger at the injustice of these women having been abused and then punished–in many cases for doing something to end the abuse.

But then the mental tape in my head would flip, and I would switch from thoughts of anger to thoughts of *how brave she was. What courage that woman had to pick up that phone and dial that hotline number and talk to a total stranger. She had no idea where the shelter was.* Many women shared their stories with me of tiptoeing out of the house in the middle of the night while whispering to the kids, "Don't wake him up." Leaving takes an enormous amount of courage. I had immediate admiration for every woman that walked through the door of the shelter— especially if she had little kids with her — because I could only imagine how hard it was to leave her home with no money, with only the clothes on her back, and jump into the unknown.

Am I that courageous? I don't know. I've never been tested. The hardest thing I've had to do was move my family of seven across the country five times in five years when my children were young, due to my husband's career in real estate. But we were moving together as a family, and always had a home to go to. I've never had to leave my home in the middle of the night in order to protect myself or my children. I've never been slapped or pushed or beaten.

The women I've come to know at the shelter and in the L.I.F.E. Group at ORW in Marysville have taught me what resilience and strength look like. Under the most difficult conditions, many of them have come to live lives of compassion, service to others, hard work, acceptance, and forgiveness. They have my utmost respect and love. They are my sisters.

Appendix

Domestic Violence—By the Numbers

- Every 9 seconds, a woman in the United States is assaulted or beaten.[1]

- One in three women has experienced physical violence by an intimate partner.[2]

- In the early 1990s, the Center for Disease Control and Prevention stated that domestic violence was the number one cause of injury and the number one public health threat for women in America.[3]

- Eighty-five percent of domestic violence victims are women.[4]

- Up to 6 million women are believed to be beaten in their homes each year.[5]

- Violence against women occurs predominantly behind closed doors at home with most cases having never been reported to police.[6]

- On average, three women are killed every day by a partner or former partner.[7]

- On a typical day, there are more than 20,000 phone calls placed to domestic violence hotlines nationwide.[8]

- Domestic violence happens to people in all walks of life regardless of age, gender, sexual orientation, race, religion, education, profession or socioeconomic status.[9]

- Approximately one-third of the men counseled (for battering) are professional men who are well respected in their jobs and their communities. These batterers included doctors, psychologists, lawyers, ministers, and business executives.[10]

Shelters

- There are over 20,000 cities and towns in America, but only 1,300 battered women's shelters.[11]

- There are 3 times as many animal shelters in the United States than battered women's shelters.[12]

- In just one day in 2015, over 31,500 adults and children fleeing domestic violence found refuge in a domestic violence emergency shelter or transitional housing program.[13]

- That same day, domestic violence programs were unable to meet over 12,197 requests for services because of a lack of funding, staffing, or other resources.[14]

- Emergency shelter and transitional housing continue to be the most urgent unmet needs for domestic violence survivors.[15]

Domestic Violence, Children, and Homelessness

- The biggest predictive indicator for someone becoming an abuser is exposure to it as a child.[16]

- An estimated 3.3 million children in the U.S. each year witness violence against their mother or female caretaker by a family member.[17]

- 40-60% of men who abuse women also abuse children.[18]

- One in 5 teenage girls say they have been in a relationship where the boyfriend threatened violence or self-harm if a breakup was to occur.[19]

- Nationally, 50% of all homeless women and children are on the streets because of violence in the home.[20]

- Domestic violence is the third leading cause of homelessness among families.[21]

Economic Impact of Domestic Violence

- Victims of intimate partner violence lose a total of eight million days of paid work each year.[22]

- Intimate partner violence is estimated to cost the US economy between $5.8 billion and $12.6 billion annually.[23]

- Between 21-60% of victims of intimate partner violence lose their jobs due to reasons stemming from the abuse.[24]

Domestic Violence and Health

- Four million women require police or medical attention each year due to severe beatings.[25]

- 40-70% of female murder victims in the U.S. are killed by their husbands or boyfriends, often within an ongoing abusive relationship.[26]

- On average, more than three women a day are murdered by their husbands or boyfriends in the United States.[27]

- The presence of a gun in a domestic violence situation increases the risk of homicide by 500%.[28]

- According to the American Medical Association, family violence kills as many women every 5 years as the total number of Americans who died in the Vietnam War.[29]

- The U.S. Surgeon General reported in 1992 that abuse by a partner is the leading cause of injury to American women between age 15 and 41.[30]

- Domestic victimization is correlated with a higher rate of depression and suicidal behavior.[31]

- Only 34% of people who are injured by intimate partners receive medical care for their injuries.[32]

Battered Women Syndrome and Clemency

- Research has shown that "battered women who kill their abusers do so as a last resort."[33] Typically, battered women do not plan to murder their batterer, but kill them out of self-defense in the midst being attacked.[34] ... Most of the women who kill their abuser have been battered for years and finally reach a point where the beating is so bad that she believes that she would be killed if she did not kill first—either because of the intensity of the abuse or because of a previous threat made by the abuser."[35]

- The clemency movement arose in response to the "(t)he difficulties that battered women who killed their abuser encountered in receiving fair hearings on self-defense claims. … To address this injustice, women's groups across the United States organized clemency projects to attempt to reduce the sentences that battered women were given in unfair trials."[36]

- Following Ohio's lead, other states began to enact similar legislation and undergo clemency processes, including "the Framingham Eight" in Massachusetts. This movement led to the congressional passage of the Violence Against Women Act (VAWA) in 1994. This federal law protected women and children from their abusers in a myriad of ways, and prevented homicides. The VAWA expired in December 2018, and as of this writing has been reintroduced in Congress, but not passed.

- Today, battered woman syndrome is recognized as a subcategory of Post-Traumatic Stress Disorder (PTSD). The use of "battered woman syndrome" as a legal strategy has evolved to using the more inclusive term "battering and its effects" to avoid pathologizing women. This new term also recognizes that there is more than one pattern of response to battering and domestic violence.

An Abbreviated History of the Battered Women's Movement

1970   The first battered women's shelter opens in Chiswick, England, by Erin Pizzey.

1973   The first battered women's shelter in the United States opens in St. Paul, Minnesota, by the Women's Advocates.

1976   Pennsylvania establishes the first state coalition against domestic violence and becomes the first state to pass legislation providing for orders of protection for battered women. Oregon becomes the first state to legislate mandated arrest in domestic violence cases.

1978   The United States Commission on Civil Rights sponsors the Consultation on Battered Women: Issues of Public Policy in Washington, DC. Over 100 nationally represented women come together to organize around the needs of the newly formed battered women's movement. The National Coalition Against Domestic Violence (NCADV) is formed during the US Commission on Civil Rights hearing.

1979   Over 250 shelters for battered women exist in the United States.

1983   Over 700 shelters for battered women are in operation across the United States serving 91,000 women and 131,000 children.

1984   The Duluth Project is formed in Duluth, Minnesota, to develop a coordinated criminal justice response to domestic violence. The US Attorney General establishes a Task Force on Family Violence and conducts hearings throughout the country to examine the scope and nature of the problem. The report spurs Congress to pass the Family Violence Prevention Services Act – the first time federal funds are specifically designated for programs serving battered women and their children.

1985	The US Surgeon General issues a report identifying domestic violence as a major health problem for women.
1986	Battered women's shelters house over 310,000 women and children. The first Domestic Violence Awareness Month is held in October. The NCADV establishes the first national toll-free domestic violence hotline.
1989	There are 1,200 battered women's programs in the United States. US Attorney General C. Everett Koop warns that violence is the number one public health risk to adult women in the United States.
1993	Violence against women is included as a human rights violation by the United Nations at its International Conference on Human Rights in Vienna. The World Bank recognizes battering as a significant economic problem in terms of health costs.
1994	The US Congress passes the Violence Against Women Act (VAWA.) VAWA funds services for victims of domestic violence and rape, and provides training to increase police and court officials' sensitivity to domestic violence.
2000	The Violence Against Women Act of 2000 is passed reauthorizing funding for training and services for battered women and their children and creating new programs. $3.3 billion was authorized for the years 2000-2005. It was reauthorized in 2005 and 2013.
2019	The VAWA expired in December 2018, and as of this writing has been reintroduced in Congress, but not passed.

Ways to Help

National Domestic Violence Hotline
800-799-7233 / 800-787-3224 (TTY)

Have this number in your contacts to give to someone. They can help in learning the warning signs and provide advice and guidance on how to help if you think you or someone you know is being abused physically, emotionally or financially.

Believe survivors, and be a safe person for them to talk to. Survivors are frequently isolated from any support networks as part of the abuse. Having a friend or advocate they can confide in can make all the difference in a person's journey to safety.

Research your state legislation, existing and pending, relating to domestic violence. Write your state legislators for stricter domestic violence laws, especially if your state has not yet enacted legislation to classify choking and strangulation as felonies (as of January 2019 Ohio, Kentucky, North Dakota, South Carolina, Maryland have yet to do this.)

Write or call elected representatives in Washington, DC urging them to pass the newly reintroduced Violence Against Women Act. Ask that it be passed with no expiration date.

A quick and easy way to learn about pending legislation and contact your elected officials is to go the National Network to End Domestic Violence's (NNEDV) Take Action Center at https://nnedv.org/policy-center/action-center/

October is Domestic Violence Awareness month. Learn what is happening in your area that you can support and participate in.

Volunteer: Locate shelters near you via domesticshelters.org (as listed below.)

Donate: Monetary donations can be made via the National Coalition Against Domestic Violence website: http://ncadv.org

Donate items to shelters:

https://www.domesticshelters.org/fundraisers/wish-lists#.WMyIYzvys2w

https://www.simplemost.com/12-things-local-womens-shelter-desperately-needs/

Check your local area for additional resources and organizations.

Appendix Endnotes

1. https://domesticviolencestatistics.org/domestic-violence-statistics/

2. National Center for Disease Control "The National Intimate Partner and Sexual Violence Survey 2010" https://www.cdc.gov/violenceprevention/pdf/nisvs_report2010-a.pdf

   National Coalition Against Domestic Violence: Statistics

   https://ncadv.org/statistics

3. Lazarus, Margaret and Renner Wunderlich. 1994. *Defending Our Lives.* Cambridge: Cambridge Documentary Films, Inc. Cited in Schornstein, Jackie, *Lessons from the Past: Revitalizing the Clemency Movement for Battered Women Incarcerated for Killing Their Abuser in* Women Leading Change © Newcomb College Institute, 2016, Vol. I, Issue no. 1, p. 81.

4. "30 Shocking Domestic Violence Statistics That Remind Us It's An Epidemic" Huffington Post December 06, 2017. Retrieved from

   https://www.huffingtonpost.com/2014/10/23/domestic-violence-statistics_n_5959776.html

5. Beacon of Hope Crisis Center "Domestic Violence Statistics" https://beaconofhopeindy.org/domestic-violence-statistics.html

6. domesticshelters.org: "Domestic Violence Statistics: The hard truth about domestic violence"

   https://www.domesticshelters.org/articles/statistics/domestic-violence-statistics

7. "30 Shocking Domestic Violence Statistics That Remind Us It's An Epidemic" Huffington Post December 06, 2017. Retrieved from

https://www.huffingtonpost.com/2014/10/23/domestic-violence-statistics_n_5959776.html

8. National Coalition Against Domestic Violence: Statistics https://ncadv.org/statistics

9. domesticshelters.org: "Domestic Violence Statistics: The hard truth about domestic violence"

 https://www.domesticshelters.org/articles/statistics/domestic-violence-statistics

10. Beacon of Hope Crisis Center *Domestic Violence Statistics*

 https://beaconofhopeindy.org/domestic-violence-statistics.html

11. *Ibid.*

12. *Ibid.*

13. U.S. Department of Health and Human Services, Administration for Children and Families, Family and Youth Services Bureau: "Domestic Violence and Homelessness: Statistics (2016)"

 https://www.acf.hhs.gov/fysb/resource/dv-homelessness-stats-2016

14. *Ibid.*

15. *Ibid.*

16. *"Behind Closed Doors: The Impact of Domestic Violence on Children."* UNICEF, Child Protection Section and The Body Shop International (2006).

17. domesticshelters.org: "Domestic Violence Statistics: The hard truth about domestic violence" May 1, 2014 https://www.domesticshelters.org/articles/faq/domestic-violence-statistics

18. *Ibid.*

19. *Ibid.*

20. Beacon of Hope Crisis Center *Domestic Violence Statistics*

 https://beaconofhopeindy.org/domestic-violence-statistics.html

21. U.S. Department of Health and Human Services, Administration for Children and Families, Family and Youth Services Bureau: Domestic Violence and Homelessness

 https://www.acf.hhs.gov/domestic-violence-and-homelessness

22. National Coalition Against Domestic Violence https://www.speakcdn. com/assets/2497/domestic_violence2.pdf

23. *Ibid.*

24. *Ibid.*

25. Beacon of Hope Crisis Center "Domestic Violence Statistics" https:// beaconofhopeindy.org/domestic-violence-statistics.html

26. domesticshelters.org: "Domestic Violence Statistics: The hard truth about domestic violence" May 1, 2014 https://www.domesticshelters. org/articles/statistics/domestic-violence-statistics

27. American Psychological Association, *Intimate Partner Violence Facts and Resources* https://www.apa.org/topics/violence/partner

28. The National Domestic Violence Hotline https://www.thehotline.org/ resources/firearms-dv/

29. Beacon of Hope Crisis Center "Domestic Violence Statistics" https:// beaconofhopeindy.org/domestic-violence-statistics.html

30. *Ibid.*

31. National Coalition Against Domestic Violence https://www.speakcdn. com/assets/2497/domestic_violence2.pdf

32. U.S. Department of Justice, Bureau of Justice Statistics, *Special Report on Nonfatal Domestic Violence, 2003-2012, p. 8.* https://www.bjs.gov/ content/pub/pdf/ndv0312.pdf

33. Hawes, Matthew *Removing the Roadblocks to Successful Domestic Violence Prosecutions:*, 53 Cleveland State Law Review 133 (2005-2006).

34. Schornstein, Jackie *Lessons from the Past: Revitalizing the Clemency Movement for Battered Women Incarcerated for Killing Their Abuser in* Women Leading Change © Newcomb College Institute, 2016, Vol. I, Issue no. 1, p. 78.

35. Goodmark, Leigh. 2006. "The Punishment of Dixie Shanahan: Is There Justice for Battered Women Who Kill?" Bepress Legal Series, Paper 1128, p. 14. Cited in Schornstein, p. 81.

36. Schornstein, p. 8

Sammy Dyer

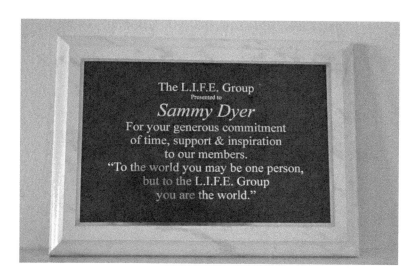

Acknowledgments

Thank you to Joe Clark and Mary Dwyer for steadfast commitment to the cause, and for your friendship over all these years.

Thank you to Becky Cardine for your vision and determination in the early days of the L.I.F.E. Group, and for sharing your memories.

Thank you to Clara Golding-Kent for your unwavering and compassionate commitment to the L.I.F.E. Group, and for your help in compiling information for this book.

Thank you to Josephine Adkins for sharing your strength and courage, and for your inspirational force in my life. Your dedication to helping victims of domestic violence reflects the true meaning of leading by example.

Thank you to Vanessa Buffington for your courage and willingness to share your story. Your grace and dignity in accepting your life as it is and building the best life you can is deserving of the utmost respect. You are and will remain my very dear friend.

Thank you to former Ohio First Lady Dagmar Celeste and former Ohio State Representative Joe Koziura for inspiration and leadership in the effort to help victims of domestic violence.

Thank you to Chrissa Pederson for careful reading and skillful editing of the draft manuscript.

Thank you to Margy Klaw for helpful feedback and suggestions in the early stages.

Thank you to Katie Young-Wildes at Women Against Abuse for feedback and suggestions on the "Ways to Help" page.

Thank you to Bill Wilkinson, Katie Wilkinson, and Mary Grace Wilkinson for love, support, and encouragement from the start.

About the Authors

Sammy Dyer, at age 88, continues to advocate for victims of domestic violence and incarcerated women. A former kindergarten teacher and mother of five, she worked full time for over 20 years as a guardianship assistant for an elder-care and estate planning attorney. She reluctantly retired at the age of 86, but continues her work advocating for battered and incarcerated women, and attends monthly L.I.F.E Group meetings at the Ohio Reformatory for Women.

Deb Dyer, Sammy Dyer, and Mary Dyer Wilkinson

In addition to her work with battered women, raising five kids, and having a full-time job, Sammy volunteered in the Child Life Department at Cleveland Metropolitan General Hospital for nearly 30 years. Her commitment to volunteer work has been recognized with numerous volunteer service awards, and by the fact that when she enters the room at the monthly L.I.F.E. Group meeting, her "sisters" stand and cheer. Her dedication, compassion and love for the women she has worked with has been passed down to her children and grandchildren.

Deb Dyer is the author, along with her sister Mary Dyer Wilkinson, of the stage play and adapted screenplay "The Unexpected Advocate," a fictionalized account of an enduring friendship between their mother and one woman from a battered women's shelter. e play was awarded third place in the 2018 New Works of Merit The International Playwriting competition. She shares her mother and sister's commitment to raising awareness about domestic violence, and is honored to do so through this work.

Deb studied European history at the University of Pennsylvania and has had an eclectic career path. She has been a life guard, bartender, Peace Corps Volunteer, hotel manager, certified therapeutic horse-back riding instructor, ultimately settling into the equestrian industry training horses and riders while managing and consulting for equestrian facilities. She has lived in Michigan, California, Georgia, Africa, the Maldive Islands, Key West, Pennsylvania, South Carolina and Ohio, although not necessarily in that order.

Mary Dyer Wilkinson has co-written the stage play "The Unexpected Advocate" with her sister, Deb Dyer. She shares her mother's commitment to volunteer work and helping those less fortunate. Her family developed the Rose Fischer Wilkinson Foundation to help those in need in times of pain, crisis and personal tragedy.

Mary has worked in Higher Education for over 25 years, helping college students achieve their academic dreams. In addition to her volunteer work with the Rose Fischer Wilkinson Foundation, Mary spends time fundraising and supporting the arts in her community. Her husband and two daughters are always in her corner, supporting her initiatives and endeavors.

Linda Hansell is a writer and educator based in Philadelphia, Pennsylvania. Her co-written books include *Dancing in the Wonder for 102 Years* and *Memories of a Life*. Her essays have been published in the *Emerald Coast Review*, *Months to Years*, and *Wising Up Press*.

Linda has over thirty years of experience teaching and designing educational programs for under-served students of all

Linda Hansell

ages. Linda holds a Ph.D. in Education from the University of Pennsylvania, and a B.A. in Philosophy from Williams College.

Linda has known and admired Sammy Dyer since she became life-long friends with Sammy's oldest daughter when they were in Kindergarten. Linda is thrilled to be helping tell the story of this remarkable woman. Linda's website is

https://lindahansellwriter.squarespace.com

Made in USA - North Chelmsford, MA
1062752_9781951896041
03.25.2020 1217